THE *CEO Contract:*

A GUIDE FOR PRESIDENTS AND BOARDS
2nd Edition

THE *CEO Contract:*

A GUIDE FOR PRESIDENTS AND BOARDS
2nd Edition

DESNA L. WALLIN

Foreword by George Boggs and Noah Brown

Community College Press,® a division of the American Association of Community Colleges

The American Association of Community Colleges (AACC) is the primary advocacy organization for the nation's community colleges. The association represents more than 1,200 two-year, associate degree–granting institutions and more than 11 million students. AACC promotes community colleges through six strategic action areas: national and international recognition and advocacy, learning and accountability, leadership development, economic and workforce development, connectedness across AACC membership, and international and intercultural education. Information about AACC and community colleges may be found at www.aacc.nche.edu.

Cover Design: Dodds Design
Interior Design: Gratzer Graphics LLC
Editor: Deanna D'Errico
Printer: Graphic Communications, Inc.

© 2007 American Association of Community Colleges

Community College Press
American Association of Community Colleges
One Dupont Circle, NW
Suite 410
Washington, DC 20036

Printed in the United States of America.

Library of Congress Cataloging-in-Publication Data

Wallin, Desna L.
   The CEO contract: a guide for presidents and boards / Desna L. Wallin; foreword by George Boggs and Noah Brown.—2nd ed.
      p. cm.
   Summary: "A complete guide to crafting well-written, comprehensive contracts for hiring and retaining successful community college presidents"—Provided by publisher.
   Includes bibliographical references and index.
   ISBN 978-0-87117-382-9
   1. Labor contract—United States. 2. Community college presidents—Employment—United States. I. Title.

KF898.W35 2007
378.1'11—dc22
                                              2007013376

Contents

Foreword

Community college board members are responsible for the vitality of the institutions that are central to educational opportunity for individuals and to the economic health of the community. The members are entrusted with ensuring that the college is operated effectively, efficiently, and ethically; that it is responsive to the educational and economic development needs of the community; and that planning enables the college to effectively serve future generations. Trustees neither administer the college nor draft plans for the college's future, but they see that these responsibilities are met and monitor the college's progress.

The board delegates the actual administration of the college and its internal governance and planning processes to its CEO, the board's sole employee. The term CEO as used here includes all college or district chief executives who report directly to a board, with titles including president, chancellor, superintendent/president, and director. The relationship between a board and its CEO is an important one, because neither can be very effective unless both are. It is essential that expectations are clear and that communications are regular and open. The employment agreement is an important mechanism for articulating, documenting, and monitoring these expectations. It is a legal document that should be reviewed by separate attorneys for the college and the CEO, respectively.

It is commonly said that the most important responsibility of a board is to hire a good CEO. We would argue that it is even more critical for a board to create an environment conducive to attracting the most qualified candidate and retaining a peak-performing CEO. In that regard, the CEO employment agreement is a tool for fulfilling the board's responsibility to the community.

The agreement serves as a written record and can be used to prevent misunderstandings between the CEO and the board during the CEO's tenure and upon termination. The agreement should clearly state the terms of employment, including duties, salary, benefits, expense allowances, working conditions, and term of office. It should also include a process for regular performance evaluation and specify the board's role in monitoring performance. CEOs and boards should never agree to any benefit that is not included in writing in the employment agreement.

Most CEO candidates will ask about the college environment. What was the relationship between the board and the outgoing CEO? Was the board clear in its expectations and communications? Are there issues or problems that the board wants the new CEO to address? Does the board respect the boundaries between policy setting and administration—that is, will the board let the CEO do the job? In other words, candidates will want to know whether the position would be good for them professionally as well as personally.

To attract the best candidates, a wise board will offer a competitive employment package with an array of standard and enhanced benefits. Both boards and CEOs should be aware that there is no one employment agreement that would apply in all situations. The circumstances of each CEO are different. Each is at a different life and career stage, and the agreement should be crafted to address those differences. For example, CEOs who are moving from one state to another may need help to recover lost retirement benefits. Young CEOs may need help with child care. If a CEO would be moving into a more expensive housing area, the employment agreement may need to address housing.

We also caution boards not to discount the value of a CEO based on gender or ethnicity. While it is still an unfortunate fact that minorities and women, on average, receive statistically lower compensation and benefits in the U.S. workforce, community colleges must set the example for equity.

Excellent CEOs are often recruited for new positions. While it may be positive for both a CEO and a college to have a change, a board has an obligation to ensure that the reasons for potential separation are not related to weaknesses in the employment agreement. The cost of replacing a CEO can be significant, and the loss of an experienced and effective CEO can be difficult for both the college and the community, as well as undermine the community's confidence in the board and the college.

The employment agreement is a living document that should be updated and kept competitive over the long term. While a board might take fiduciary satisfaction in keeping compensation and benefits to a minimum, the cost of replacing a CEO will more than likely make up for any savings, and increasing compensation to attract qualified replacement candidates might be politically more difficult than periodically reviewing and updating the current CEO's compensation. Adjustments to the employment agreement should be discussed with the CEO annually. Annual performance reviews should also be scheduled to assess progress toward meeting college goals, to clarify expectations, and to recognize accomplishments.

Creating and maintaining an environment that enables the CEO to be successful is a board responsibility that requires continued attention. CEOs must feel safe to take risks and to make decisions that are difficult and not always popular. Multiyear employment contracts provide the security that a CEO needs to be the most effective leader, and they show the board's confidence in the CEO. Boards should not fall into the trap of thinking that their college is so good that there will not be difficult leadership problems. Every college experiences problems, and leaders who are confident in their abilities and sure of their positions are best equipped to address them.

Community college CEOs are often expected to interact with other leaders in the community and to serve with them on boards and committees. The college CEO should be seen as someone who is as important to the community as is the local hospital administrator, school superintendent, or city or county official. Local media often report the compensation and benefit packages for public community college CEOs, and such public reporting can send a message about the relative importance of the CEO in the community. Provisions in the employment agreement can make it possible for the CEO to support local charitable events and causes and to become a member of local clubs.

Boards also have an obligation to encourage the CEO to grow professionally. The employment agreement should provide for the professional development of the CEO, reimbursing costs for professional travel, conference attendance, and institutes or workshops. Boards should resist arguments to limit the travel expense reimbursement of the CEO to that of other employees—more is expected of the CEO, and what the CEO does affects every other employee. CEOs should also be encouraged to take vacation days and periodic paid leaves of absence so they maintain their health and enthusiasm.

The tenure of even the best CEO eventually comes to an end. Intention to separate from employment can originate from either the CEO or the board, but it is preferable that separations, in the end, are by mutual agreement. The CEO may want to retire or accept another position. Sometimes CEOs realize that the job they came to do is completed, and the institution has moved to a point where new leadership is needed. Sometimes a CEO wants a different level of challenge. If the CEO has served the college well, the board should publicly acknowledge and reward the contributions. Boards should not feel betrayed by a CEO who has made a contribution and now wants to explore other opportunities or to retire.

Likewise, if a board decides it is time for new leadership, it is desirable to reach a mutual agreement for separation. CEOs should be given an opportunity to leave with dignity, with their professional reputations intact, and in a position to seek new leadership positions. We have seen too many cases of acrimonious dismissals of CEOs in which allegations are reported prominently in local and national press. These contentious separations damage the reputations of the board, the CEO, and the college. They make it difficult for the CEO to secure another leadership position and difficult for the college to recruit a replacement. When necessary, a mediator should be employed to negotiate a separation agreement. However, a well-written separation clause in the employment agreement may prevent these difficult situations.

Community college leadership is both challenging and complex. It requires a trusting and mutually supportive relationship between a board of trustees and a CEO. Well-written employment agreements play an important role in clarifying expectations from the outset and in establishing the environment for effective leadership. We hope this publication assists both boards and CEOs in the preparation and review of these important living documents.

George R. Boggs
President and CEO
American Association of Community Colleges

J. Noah Brown
President and CEO
Association of Community College Trustees

Preface

Being a successful community college president today requires having the courage and determination to face increasing competition and demands that community colleges do things better, faster, and cheaper. Boards want presidents who are creative, innovative, and willing to take risks to solve complex problems. A well-drafted employment agreement provides the incentive, security, and stability necessary for a CEO to move the institution forward. It defines how the board nurtures, encourages, manages, and supports the president. It defines the expectations by presidents for some reasonable level of security and stability in their careers. It is a "partnership of responsibilities" between the CEO of a community college and its board of trustees.

When the American Association of Community Colleges (AACC) and the Association of Community College Trustees (ACCT) first discussed the need for a book on CEO employment agreements, we had no idea of the groundbreaking contribution Desna Wallin would make to community colleges. The first edition proved to be an essential resource for boards and presidents who wanted to promote strong and effective relationships. The book was extremely well received and proved to be a valuable tool for presidents and for boards of trustees embarking in negotiating a new contract or renewing an existing contract.

Drawing on the experience of presidents throughout the country, her own research, and her decades of experience, Wallin persuasively demonstrates the value of a well-crafted employment agreement. She illustrates the complexity of the CEO position and how best to position the president for success. The second edition of *The CEO Contract: A Guide for Presidents and Boards* is indispensable for boards who want to define standards of accountability and to properly compensate and reward exemplary leaders. Each of the 6,500 elected and appointed trustees who serve our community colleges should have a copy of this book; it should be required reading for the board's attorney.

To augment the valuable information provided in this edition, we offer the following advice, based on our experience working with elected and appointed boards of trustees across the country.

Assume full responsibility for enforcing the contract. The board's responsibilities include ensuring that all aspects of the negotiated contract resulting from the employment agreement are executed and honored. Do not delegate that responsibility to the president. Doing so can put the president in an uncomfortable and difficult situation. Plan appropriately and follow a timetable for renewing the contract. We recommend that the review and renewal of the contract is incorporated into the board's annual calendar and that the board dedicate all the time necessary to address this important responsibility.

Involve all board members in the process. The responsibility for negotiating or renewing the contract with the president rests with the full board. Board leaders should take steps to provide opportunities for all board members to be involved. The process should not be rushed and should allow time for discussion and questions. Keep in mind that all board members may not have extensive experience negotiating executive contracts; therefore, extra care should be taken to ensure that all members are familiar with all aspects of the employment agreement and are prepared to honor its terms. It is the board's responsibility to make sure that each trustee is fully aware of the terms.

Keep the president informed and involved. The board must keep the president informed and should follow the "no surprises" rule. Any concerns should be openly discussed with the president. A good relationship with a successful president can be weakened and put at risk if the board decides to modify the terms of the employment agreement without extending the president the courtesy of a full discussion.

Be well informed. By comparing salaries, benefits, and lengths of terms across states and regions, board members will not only gain a better understanding of the marketplace, but also they will be in a better position to offer a competitive package. State associations and ACCT are good sources of accurate and impartial information. Being well informed will also enable the board to react and respond to scrutiny from the public and to defend its actions, if needed.

Be prepared to share information with the public. The board's response to external questioning may influence how internal and external constituencies judge the start of the new presidency or support for a current president. Therefore, it is imperative to understand and appreciate the demands of the presidency. The board's role includes educating the public about and celebrating the accomplishments of the president.

Seek appropriate legal advice. We encourage the board to consult legal counsel that has significant experience in contract development to draft or review contracts. This point is made throughout the book, but it is important enough to bear repeating. The board should also encourage the president to have his or her own legal counsel review the agreement before it is signed. Both parties should enter into the relationship with a full understanding of the formal agreement. A new presidency typically begins with good will and excitement, so it is the best time to ensure that the agreement provides the foundation for a cooperative relationship and that it is fair to both parties.

Presidential search provides an opportunity to build a CEO contract. An important part of the search for the new president is the negotiation and preparation of the employment agreement. Boards need to be concerned about all aspects of the search and selection process including how the contract will be prepared, negotiated, and approved. Do not wait until you are ready to select a final candidate to start considering the contract preparation process.

Develop an evaluation process for CEOs and the board. Investing in an evaluation process is prudent. Evaluations should be conducted in a timely, fair, and professional manner and should involve the entire board. We recommend that the board participate in a retreat or, at a minimum, set aside enough time to have a full review and performance discussion with the president. The board should provide the president with written goals, priorities, and expectations and use this as the basis for evaluating performance. We also encourage the board to plan in advance for incorporating self-assessment of its performance into the discussion.

Although good employment agreements and contracts cannot guarantee good relationships between boards and presidents, the process of negotiating and crafting a contract is an important first step toward solidifying a good relationship. The process gives all parties the opportunity to forge a relationship that is based on mutual respect, common goals, accountability, and an unselfish desire to provide strong leadership. A well-crafted employment agreement provides both parties with clear expectations, accountability measures, the tools to reinforce and reward great performance, and an exit strategy when necessary. The review and renewal of the contract should be a top priority for the board. Remember: There is no substitute for valuing and rewarding performance.

Narcisa A. Polonio
Vice President of Board Leadership Services
Association of Community College Trustees

Lynda Stanley
Chair, ACCT Board of Directors
Trustee, Brunswick Community College, NC

Acknowledgments

No author writes a book in isolation. I am particularly grateful for the leadership provided by George Boggs, president and CEO of the American Association of Community Colleges (AACC), and Noah Brown, president and CEO of the Association of Community College Trustees (ACCT), for their interest in and encouragement of the project. Many AACC staff members provided invaluable service as well. Of special note is the research data assistance provided by Kent Phillippe, Courtney Larson, and Jeff Mills. Margaret Rivera and Mary Ann Settlemire gave useful suggestions for both content and format. Norma Kent and Deanna D'Errico provided editorial leadership and guidance.

Narcisa Polonio of ACCT gave welcome insights from the board perspective. The case study contributed by Paul Elsner, chancellor emeritus of the Maricopa County Community College district, added another dimension and understanding to contract development, which should be very useful to both boards and CEOs.

The comments and suggestions of the 548 CEOs from across the country who responded to the survey added a great deal of depth and real-world experience to the book. Of special note are those presidents who openly shared not only their contracts but also their positive and negative experiences in negotiating those contracts. Their perspectives as shared in the book will be appreciated by colleagues across the country who are able to gain practical insights from the experiences of these presidents.

I also owe a debt of gratitude to Ron Cervero, chair of the Department of Lifelong Education, Administration, and Policy at the University of Georgia. He understood the importance of a flexible schedule necessary for writing and offered encouragement and support throughout the process.

Finally, my greatest debt is to my husband, Harry Jarrett, whose experience, patience, thoughtful suggestions, and endless pots of coffee helped make the book a reality.

Desna L. Wallin

Introduction

The revised and expanded second edition of *The CEO Contract: A Guide for Presidents and Boards* builds on the success and usefulness of the 2003 edition. Feedback from the first book indicated that it was informative and practical and appreciated by both boards and presidents. At the urging of participants at the 2006 Presidents Academy in Kennebunkport and participants at the 2006 Leadership Congress of the Association of Community College Trustees (ACCT) in Orlando, George Boggs and other leaders at the American Association of Community Colleges (AACC) decided that an update would be timely and appropriate. Thus, a new electronic survey was developed and sent to member presidents and chancellors in October 2006. The findings from that survey provide the foundation for this revised and updated second edition. In addition to updated survey results, the second edition contains new chapters on ethics and on arbitration and mediation. An expanded discussion of various types of compensation and benefits is presented, examples from the field are highlighted, and direct quotations from survey respondents are used.

This book is intended to provide governing boards and CEOs with a framework they can use to develop successful and effective employment agreements. Using this framework, they can engage in a communication process that results in clear expectations, meaningful assessment, mutual respect and understanding, and graceful and dignified exit strategies for the benefit of the president, the board, and the institution. *The CEO Contract: A Guide for Presidents and Boards* is intended to provide an understanding of options, alternatives, best practices, and perhaps some examples of what *not* to do. It is not a form book from which a board or CEO can create an agreement.

If there is one overarching theme in college executive employment agreements, it is that one size does not fit all. A wide variety of factors influence the form and nature of an agreement. Some are obvious, such as regional differences in compensation patterns or what is expected of the chancellor of a large multicampus system; the president of a unionized, urban institution; and the president of a small, rural college. The agreement between the governing board and the CEO should reflect the culture of the institution and its environment, as well as comport with the requirements of law under which the institution operates. The agreement between an institution and its CEO is not only a very important document, but also it describes a complex set of legally enforceable rights and obligations. It is a *contract*, with all of the legal nuances that accompany that term.

NO GOVERNING BOARD OR PROSPECTIVE CEO SHOULD EVER ENTER INTO AN EMPLOYMENT AGREEMENT, WHICH IS A CONTRACT, WITHOUT FIRST OBTAINING COMPETENT LEGAL ADVICE.

Employment agreements are governed by a complex web of federal and state law and regulation, as well as more than 200 years of judicial decisions. A provision that works perfectly well in one state might well prove unenforceable in another. An institution that operates more directly as an entity of a state may have different options in negotiating an agreement than does one that is considered part of a county or city. The nuances are many—and far beyond the scope of this book.

This book provides a starting point from which boards and prospective CEOs can glean ideas, approaches, practices, and pitfalls. But no executive employment agreement should ever be brought to the desired end (that is, signed by all parties) without careful and thorough review by experienced counsel, separately advising the board and the candidate. It is true that good legal advice can be expensive. It is also true that the costs of a badly or improperly drafted agreement can be disastrous. Readers are advised that this book is not intended to and does not offer legal advice. Competent counsel should always be consulted before entering into any legally binding agreements.

CONTENT

The book contains 11 chapters. In the first chapter, "The Presidency," the nature of the position in the first decade of the 21st century is examined. Changes in the demographics of colleges and boards and the professionalization of the position have made it increasingly important for boards and presidents to be knowledgeable about the nature of compensation and the desirability of clear employment agreements.

In chapter 2, the basic components of an employment agreement are presented, and the advantages and disadvantages of such a contractual arrangement are discussed. The importance of a well-informed compensation committee is also discussed. In chapter 3, the term of appointment is reviewed. There are a variety of arrangements—from "at the pleasure of the board" to an indefinite time in the distant future—for the term of appointment. However, the most common contracts are for a term of 3 years, and many are now incorporating rollover provisions.

Nothing is more important to the success of a CEO than a clear set of expectations by which his or her tenure will be judged. In chapter 4, the importance of well-thought-out expectations and assessments are discussed. Evaluations of CEOs need to be handled with sensitivity, and the results should increase the level of understanding and communication between a board and the president. The future direction of the college and decisions concerning future compensation are all linked to evaluations of the CEO.

In chapter 5, compensation issues are discussed, including base salary, raises, bonuses, supplements, outside income, and retirement income. In chapter 6, details on standard benefits are provided, including insurance, leave provisions, car expenses, relocation and moving expenses, and professional development. In chapter 7, enhanced benefits are addressed. These include important considerations such as housing, entertainment expenses, club memberships, charitable contributions, technology and communication, and other benefits specific to the needs of a president.

In chapter 8, the all-important termination clause is examined. It is an area that new presidents in particular may be reluctant to approach, but one that requires careful attention and planning. Different types of termination, issues of notice and compensation, and extension of benefits are reviewed. The case study in chapter 9, contributed by Paul Elsner, chancellor emeritus of the Maricopa County Community College system, presents the possibilities of mediation and arbitration, important alternatives to unproductive and expensive litigation. In chapter 10, the significance of professional ethics practiced proactively by both the CEO and the board are examined. Finally, in chapter 11, important concepts presented in previous chapters are reviewed, and conclusions and recommendations are presented for a board and a president as they pursue the development of an effective employment agreement that will contribute to a successful presidential tenure.

METHODOLOGY

The preparation of the book involved three distinct but interrelated activities. First, a review of the existing literature was conducted. Second, an e-mail survey titled the CEO Contract and Compensation Survey (CCCS) was developed and piloted. The survey was then distributed to 1,018 community college presidents and chancellors. Presidents and chancellors of institutional members of AACC served as the population for this study. The survey questions elicited information on duties and responsibilities, term of the contract, compensation, evaluation, benefits, termination, and retirement. Two follow-up reminders were sent. A total of 548 usable survey replies were received, for a response rate of 54%. Not every question was answered by all respondents; thus, in determining percentages, only the number of responses to each question was used. A copy of the survey is included in the appendix. Third, actual employment contracts provided by current presidents were reviewed to determine the various ways in which boards and presidents put in writing their mutual understanding of the role, responsibility, compensation, and evaluation of the president.

A word about terminology and definitions is in order. *CCCS* refers to the survey instrument, the CEO Contract and Compensation Survey, sent to all AACC member presidents and chancellors. The term *board* is used to signify the governing authority of the institution or system, whose members may be elected or appointed. The terms *CEO* and *president* are used interchangeably to mean the person charged with the authority and responsibility for college leadership and operational decisions. Other titles, including chancellor, provost, and superintendent/president, have specific meaning in the context of particular states or systems. However, the term *president* is most commonly used, both in the literature and in practice in the colleges, and *CEO* is most descriptive of the complex role of the contemporary president: thus the choice of these two terms.

1 The Presidency

WHAT IS IT LIKE BEING a community college president in the early years of the 21st century? Perhaps it is not very different from the description given by Harold W. Stoke in 1959, who said that "being a college president was like a small boy walking a high picket fence—thrilled, but in constant danger of being impaled" (Kauffman, 1980, p. 9). No doubt there are few accomplishments, even that of successfully negotiating a walk on a high picket fence, that can compare with the challenge and excitement of providing presidential leadership in a community college. The experience can be incredibly exhilarating and rewarding, as well as challenging and exhausting.

Barwick (2002) made the point that the community college presidency has come to rival issues such as teaching and learning in the attention it has recently garnered in the scholarly literature and the popular press. Most research, he went on to say, emphasizes one of the following arguments concerning the nature of the contemporary college presidency: "(1) We are at the brink of crisis because presidents will be retiring faster than the available applicant pool can fill the vacancies and (2) The job has become so difficult and complex, it is a wonder any rational person would want it" (p. 7). Although the college president was once accorded "a modicum of deferential respect, he or she is now a public figure and fair game for investigative reporters. And although the president may not consider himself or herself to be a politician, the position is very much in the public arena" (Davis & Davis, 1999, p. 126).

THE FUTURE

It has been well documented that large numbers of presidents will be retiring in the next few years (King, 2007; Shults, 2001). The growth spurt that accompanied the establishment and rapid growth of community colleges in the 1960s and 1970s portends a significant number of retirements in the first decade of the 21st century (Campbell, 2002). It is also indisputable that the presidency of a community college is an extremely demanding role. According to Vaughan and Weisman (1998), more than 91% of then-current presidents said that they spent in excess of 50 hours a week on college work. Perhaps not surprising is the fact that 69% of those presidents who took a vacation of at least 2 weeks reported that they did college work while on vacation. In fact, administration in general has become less attractive as a career choice. In a discussion of leadership challenges in secondary education, Zirkle and Cotton (2001) pointed to a dilemma that is also apparent in higher education: "All of this to enter an administrative area that demands longer hours, places more stress, and offers fewer rewards than the teaching profession. It is not a bright prospect" (p. 17).

In 2006 the Association of Governing Boards of Universities and Colleges (AGB) Task Force on the State of the Presidency in American Higher Education released a report that questioned whether or not colleges would be able to attract high-caliber leaders to the presidency because of the external and internal challenges and conflicting pressures that a president must deal with on a daily basis. The report emphasized the need for boards and presidents to work together in a "new style of collaborative but decisive leadership" characterized as integral leadership. This new leadership links "the president, the faculty, and the board together in a well-functioning partnership purposefully devoted to a well-defined, broadly affirmed institutional vision" (AGB Task Force, 2006, p. vii). Mutually reinforcing leadership from the board and the president may make the presidency more attractive to those upcoming leaders who are debating whether or not to move from their comfortable senior leadership role to the more challenging and visible role of a CEO.

Although it is well documented that there is a diminishing supply of sitting presidents, there is also an increasingly small number of those who would ordinarily replace them: the vice presidents and deans (Shults, 2001). The author of the American Council on Education study, *The American College President: 2007 Edition* (King, 2007), suggested that the council intends to do a basic demographic study to see whether other members of the college administrative team are also aging. King further addressed the pipeline issue in an interview with the *Chronicle of Higher Education:* "If the provosts and other senior-level people are moving toward retirement, too, that's a big issue" (cited in June, 2007, p. A3). Many of the people in these senior-level positions are also nearing retirement and are leaving the profession at almost the same rate as are presidents. The pipeline is diminishing.

SKILLS AND COMPETENCIES

The skills that are required of today's president are more far-reaching and complex than those required only a decade or two ago. In Vaughan and Weisman's 1998 study, sitting community college presidents identified some of the skills that they believed would be important to future community college presidents. Those skills include the following:

- ability to bring all segments of the college into the governing process

- aptitude for building consensus

- understanding of technology

- high tolerance for ambiguity

- appreciation of multiculturalism

- ability to build successful partnerships and coalitions

In a 2002 study of the professional development needs of presidents in three states—North Carolina, South Carolina, and Georgia—presidents were asked to give their perceptions of additional skills, beyond conventional leadership skills, that were needed by a 21st-century community college president (Wallin, 2002). The responses included team development, wise delegation, common sense, oral presentation skills, fundraising ability, political savvy, vision for the college, decision-making and problem-solving skills, and moral and ethical leadership. It was also noted that golf was a useful skill as was the "tenacity of a bulldog, hide of an elephant, stomach of a goat, disposition of a jackass, and public image of Mother Teresa!" (Wallin, 2002, p. 32).

In 2005, AACC released the results of a Kellogg Foundation–funded multiyear project titled Leading Forward (Ottenritter, 2006). This project focused on developing a framework of skills and competencies needed by contemporary community college leaders. After an intensive process involving more than 100 community college leaders in a variety of educational summits, six essential competencies, with accompanying illustrations and examples, were identified. These six competencies are as follows:

- Organizational strategy—strategically improves quality, protects long-term health, promotes success of students, and sustains the community college mission.

- Resource management—equitably and ethically sustains people, processes, information, and physical and financial assets.

- Communication—uses clear listening, speaking, and writing skills to engage in honest, open dialogue at all levels of the college and community.

- Collaboration—develops and maintains responsive, cooperative, mutually beneficial, and ethical internal and external relationships.

- Community college advocacy—understands, commits to, and advocates for the mission, vision, and goals of the community college.

- Professionalism—works ethically to set high standards for self and others (Ottenritter, 2006). The skills identified by the Vaughan and Weisman study, the Wallin study, and the AACC Leading Forward project are qualitatively—and quantitatively—different from those required of community college presidents 25 or 30 years ago during the building and development mode. The demands and the expectations have escalated as the complexity and impact of the position have become more visible and as public accountability has increased.

A RISKY JOB

Successful community college leadership, then, requires a myriad of talents, persistence, commitment, and professional expertise. "As a natural consequence," Wolin suggested, "the role of the CEO involves some risk. Leading a community college is no exception. Essential to minimizing this risk is a clear understanding and agreement about expectations between a college's governing board and its CEO. Where there is a clear understanding, the CEO can pour his or her energy into planning and positive action" (Wolin, 1996, p. 1).

The perceived risk of serving in the top job at a community college has been documented by a national study of community college CEO turnover between 2003 and 2005 (Wallin & Johnson, 2006). An online survey was sent to the chief academic officers of those institutions that experienced a change in leadership in the designated time period. Among other questions, the chief academic officers were asked to judge whether or not they saw the presidency, which was the next logical career move for many of the respondents, as a risky career move. Of those responding,

57% believed that a community college presidency was indeed a "risky" career move. The reasons given varied, but they included concerns with the political nature of the job, the difficulties inherent in pleasing a variety of constituencies, budget pressures, stress levels, and the fact that "trustees can put extreme pressures on presidents that are unrealistic, such as increasing enrollments and adding programs when there are little or no resources to work with" and "micromanagement by the board." The sentiments were summed up best by one chief academic officer who said, "Because of the tenuous and political nature of the American college presidency (community college and university), a college presidency is always a 'risky' career move."

MAKING IT WORTHWHILE

With such high expectations of today's president, working in a complex and sometimes contradictory environment, it becomes more important than ever that an employment agreement be crafted that will allow a president to devote full attention and energy to the challenges at hand. There was a time, not too long ago, when a college president expected to serve "at the pleasure of the board," with the agreement sealed by a handshake. That is no longer the case for most presidents. In fact, in 1984 only 49% of the presidents at all colleges and universities had formal employment contracts; by 1997, 68% had formal contracts. By 2006, 72% of all college and university presidents had a written contract (King, 2007). For community and technical college presidents, the numbers are even higher. In 1997, 79% of public 2-year college presidents had formal, written contracts (Basinger, 2002). Data from the 2006 CCCS show that of those responding to the survey, 86% have formal written contracts or employment agreements.

Why the shift from a handshake and a promise to more formalized legal agreements? A lot of it has to do with the professionalization of the position itself. Boards, too, have become more businesslike and corporate in their orientation and expect the same of their CEOs. In the past, dealings with a board were often linked to ecclesiastical traditions—serving as the president of a university or college was actually seen as a calling. As such, the argument went, that calling should not be sullied by the ways of commerce (Basinger, 2002).

Such a mythology often resulted in considerations of financial compensation and retirement benefits being glossed over. Kauffman (1980) said quite correctly, "In the glow of having been chosen, many a candidate makes assumptions that are later mistaken. It may appear crass to raise questions of one's personal status and security when asked to be leader of a noble cause but a candidate who fails to discuss these matters often has regrets that could have been prevented" (p. 87). Nevertheless, it remains a fact that people who are drawn to the presidency are deeply committed to higher education. "Despite the changes in the marketplace, the position of college president continues to be a calling as much as a way to make a living" (Atwell & Wellman, 2000, p. v).

Sometimes a presidential candidate may avoid the subject of salary and benefits so as not to appear greedy or to stir up the press, to the detriment of both the president and the board. New presidents are sometimes hesitant to bring in an outside nego-tiator because they are afraid of damaging their future relationship with the board. Quite the contrary may actually be the case: "Instead of being offended when the president brings an experienced negotiator into the process, the board has greater respect for the president's professionalism. They would much prefer a president who knows and understands his or her limitations and seeks out expert assistance when necessary" (Cotton, 2003). The board needs to understand contract provi-sions that are common in peer institutions. State and national community college associations as well as colleges can provide a board chair and the compensation committee with the information needed to develop an initial contract or to reward an effective CEO (Nielsen & Newton, 1997). The *Chronicle of Higher Education* also compiles easily accessible and current statistics on salary and benefits of CEOs in both 4-year and 2-year institutions. A competitive compensation package is a criti-cal first step in attracting and retaining a high-performing president.

Regardless of the circumstances, "We should not expect academic leaders to take vows of poverty, nor should anyone expect them to be compensated at a com-parable level with their counterparts in the corporate sector. But somewhere in between is 'reasonable,' and each governing board must judge what is reasonable for its own institution" (Ingram, 1997, p. 10). It was said by the venerable Clark Kerr that "the ultimate test of a governing board's effectiveness is its ability to recruit and keep effective presidents" (cited in Ingram, 1997, p. 11).

It has frequently been noted that the presidency is a lonely job; only those who have been in a similar position can really understand the challenges, the disap-pointments, and the high points of such a position. This sentiment, although contemporary and accurate, is not limited to today's presidents. William Rainey Harper, the first president of the University of Chicago, wrote of this phenomenon in 1904:

Another feeling which gradually grows upon the occupant of the presidential chair is that of great loneliness—the feeling of separation from all his fellows. … the college presidency means the giving up of many things, and, not the least among them, one's most intimate friendships. Moreover, this feeling of separation, of isolation, increases with each recurring year, and, in spite of the most vigorous effort, it comes to be a thing of permanence. (cited in Kauffman, 1980, p. 89)

Although, indeed, the presidency is in many ways a lonely position, it does have its rewards. George Vaughan, professor of higher education at North Carolina State University, who served as a community college president for 17 years, has conducted many leadership seminars for those who have an interest in becoming community college presidents. As part of his presentation he discusses the pros and cons of the presidency, ending with a tongue-in-cheek observation on loneliness that goes something like this: "Yes, the presidency is a lonely position. It is lonely at the top. But I have news for you: it is lonely at the bottom, too, and the top pays more."

SUMMARY

Serving as a community college president at the beginning of the 21st century is challenging and exciting. The complexity of the job has increased significantly. Employees, the community, and business and industry all expect a college to do more at the same time that resources are diminishing. Presidents spend more hours on the job and take less vacation than they did even a decade ago. In the not-too-distant past, many presidents considered the position akin to a religious calling and, as such, were averse to being specific about the terms and conditions characteristic of a formal employment agreement. However, with the professionalization of the job of community college president, along with the increasing sophistication of governing boards, employment agreements are common: More than 86% of community college presidents had such an agreement in 2006.

The issue for boards and presidents is not so much simply having an agreement, but rather having a clear, mutually developed agreement that protects the integrity and effectiveness of the president, the board, and the college. In its 2006 report, the AGB Task Force on the State of the Presidency in American Higher Education rightly stated that "no leader comes to personify an institution in the way a president does" (p. vii). The success of the president and the success of the college are inextricably linked with the ability of the board to provide leadership in an environment of "support, candor, and accountability" (p. vii).

2 Contract Basics

WRITTEN AGREEMENTS—EITHER FORMAL CONTRACTS OR letters of appointment—are more common now. Yet some boards are still reluctant to issue a contract because they believe that it limits their authority. Others believe that only an oral agreement is necessary. The changing nature of the community college presidency, however, is making the written employment agreement increasingly important for presidents and boards.

A report issued by the Community College Leadership Development Institute in 2001 indicated that the challenges of leading a community college have become more complex and often contentious, while tenure in leadership positions has become shorter. Couple that reality with the increasingly litigious environment in which community college presidents labor, and the desirability of a formal employment agreement becomes even more obvious. In fact, boards are beginning to understand that a competitive contract may be key to attracting and retaining a quality leader.

The CCCS (AACC, 2006), conducted in conjunction with the preparation of this book, was aimed at understanding the nature of existing employment agreements and the components that make for an effective and competitive contract. (For the complete survey instrument, see the appendix.) The CCCS, sent electronically to 1,018 AACC member presidents and chancellors, resulted in 548 usable survey returns, a response rate of 54%. Although not all presidents responded to all questions, a great deal of valuable information on the state of current employment agreements was gathered.

A total of 548 presidents responded to the question "Do you have an employment contract?" Of that total, 75% said that they did have a contract, and 14% said that they did not. Of those who did not have a contract, 11% indicated that they had a letter of agreement or letter of appointment under which they operated, thus making a total of 86% of current CEOs who are working under a formal contract or letter of agreement. A smaller percentage of current presidents (14%) than presidents surveyed in 2002 (17%) were operating without any kind of formal written agreement. It appears that those who do not have a formal contract are often operating under a systemwide agreement or are in an organizational structure in which they report directly to a chancellor or system president and consequently do not have a formal contract that relates to a governing board. It is clear that there is a movement toward formalized working agreements.

When asked the reason for not having a formal employment contract, the responses were as follows: not allowed by the system (4%), not allowed by state law (2%), do not report to a board (4%), board preference (2%), and other (2%). Respondents' comments included the following:

- no written contract, work at will of chancellor, can be terminated anytime

- initial letter of appointment and then work at will

- I have an open-ended letter of agreement with only a start date. The end date is established by [state governing body] when they want me to leave.

- I serve at the pleasure of the board with no contract.

Of those without a formal contract, 9% indicated that the lack of a contract was not a concern; presumably most of those were operating under a larger system in which contracts were not permitted. Furthermore, one president indicated that the lack of a contract was by preference because that president "wanted freedom to consider other positions on occasion with[out] a contract hanging over my head." Another said, "I have tenure as a full professor." Still another said, "eligible for full retirement."

Nearly 4% indicated that they were concerned or very concerned about the lack of a contract. Comments included the following: "The chancellor has a multi-year contract, support staff have contracts, part-time employees have contracts, administrators have contracts, and faculty have contracts … but not presidents" and "I would like to have a contract." A veteran president commented, "were I earlier in my career, I would be concerned." The comment of one particularly thoughtful CEO was echoed by others and indicated concern about the importance of good legal representation: "Too few college presidents have one. Both boards and CEOs need strong legal advice for contract construction."

WHAT TO INCLUDE

What are the basic components of an employment agreement between a president and a board? Atwell and Wellman (2000) have maintained that the contract "is best confined to terms and conditions of presidential employment and should not extend to institutional plans and policy matters, though these can be referred to in the context of the presidential performance review" (p. 36). They further suggested that a basic agreement should cover four elements:

- term (duration) of the appointment

- compensation

- performance review and evaluation

- termination

The term of the appointment refers to the initial term to which the president is appointed as well as processes for extending that term. According to the survey, many CEO employment contracts are for a term of 3 to 5 years. However, the laws in some jurisdictions limit appointments to a single year, whereas some agreements provide for an indefinite term.

The compensation package includes the base salary, any provision for bonuses or other additional compensation, and a description of noneconomic benefits. The compensation package is by far the most complex component of any president's employment agreement and requires the close involvement of competent counsel. Good practice dictates that an employment agreement should provide for a clearly outlined process and timeline for the review and evaluation of the president's performance. There are many excellent published guides to assist in developing and implementing performance reviews and evaluations, including the use of goals and objectives and self-assessment instruments.

Finally, the agreement should describe the process for terminating the president's employment. "Inadequate attention to arrangements for the end of a presidency and for employment termination can place chief executives and boards in uncomfortable situations that can harm the institution. Provisions to terminate the contract should be part of the basic employment agreement" (Atwell & Wellman, 2000, p. 39).

Nason (1980) has characterized the components of a basic contract somewhat differently. He stressed that a great deal of disillusionment could be prevented if boards would be clear and specific about the "practical and professional arrangements for the new president" (p. 74). He grouped the many components of an employment agreement into three basic areas: financial, professional, and administrative.

Under the financial heading, Nason listed salary, annuity or pension provisions, medical or health insurance, life insurance, moving expenses, car expenses, travel expenses, and entertainment expenses, among others. Under professional benefits he included adequate vacation, leaves of absence, and professional competence. Under the administrative rubric he detailed items such as starting date, length of appointment, conditions of termination, criteria of performance, and provision for review and evaluation.

Perhaps how one chooses to group the elements of an employment agreement is not as important as being sure that all the important pieces are included in a way that makes sense to the board and the president and are consistent with institutional practice and state and federal law. As it has become increasingly difficult in recent years to attract the most qualified candidates, boards have come to realize the need to be more professional and businesslike to attract and retain the people they want to lead their institutions. A well-conceived employment package can significantly contribute to landing the desired candidate.

COMPENSATION COMMITTEES

In the not-so-distant past, compensation for presidents was a matter to be discussed and settled between the board chair and the president with little, if any, involvement from anyone else. However, "in today's setting, a number of factors make such a process unwise, risky, and possibly illegal for the institution and even for individual board members" (Tranquada, 2001, p. 1). Tranquada further suggested that it simply makes good sense for the compensation of the CEO, both at the initial hiring and at subsequent renewals to be

> set intelligently and responsibly with the full board's approval. The role of
> the compensation committee is to accomplish this objective in a way that pro-
> vides for all reasonable protection of the chief executive's privacy while taking

account of the significance of compensation as a means of recognizing his or her record of achievement. (Tranquada, 2001, p. 2)

A compensation committee of the board can serve a valuable function in negotiating initial and continuing contracts. It is much more efficient for the president to be dealing with a small group of board members as important compensation issues are discussed. Once the terms and conditions are agreed upon, the recommendations of the compensation committee should ordinarily be taken to the full board for ratification. (Some jurisdictions empower a compensation or executive committee to make such decisions.) At many community colleges, the board's executive committee also serves as the compensation committee. However, when the board is large, it may be more appropriate for a separate committee to focus on issues of compensation.

Regardless of the composition, it is good practice for the board chair to be actively involved, often as chair of the compensation committee. Under any circumstances, the chair should be the person who communicates the decisions of the committee to the president. However, regardless of how the board's committee structure is defined, it must be remembered that "legal authority for setting presidential compensation ultimately resides in the full board, not in a subset of its members" (AGB, 2007, p. 9).

Just what does the compensation committee do? Establishing the terms and conditions of an initial contract generally requires considerably more effort, and more involvement of outside experts, than the effort and involvement required at subsequent renewals. The compensation committee must of course negotiate the base salary, but it must also consider additional elements such as bonuses, deferred compensation, health and life insurance, car and housing allowances, travel expenses, child care, supplemental insurance, club memberships, entertainment allowances, limits on outside employment, and leave provisions. Each needs to be tailored to the specific needs of the president, the history and culture of the institution, and the overarching legal requirements imposed on the college. The compensation committee must also make clear what the evaluation and assessment process will be, including whether there will be an annual review, identified goals and objectives, and a mechanism for the board to articulate its expectations and how subsequent salary increases relate to achieving agreed-upon objectives.

The compensation committee's responsibilities change when the subject is the annual performance review. It is common practice for the board to ask the chief executive to present a self-assessment addressing previously agreed-upon goals and objectives. Likewise, board members are usually afforded the opportunity to provide their own assessments of the president's performance. The annual performance review is also the appropriate time for the board to survey the market to compare compensation packages with those of other institutions that are similar in size and mission and that are regionally comparable. Sources of information include the annual survey of compensation conducted by the *Chronicle of Higher Education*, as well as national and state professional and trustee associations. However, it must be kept in mind that these sources give only general information that is usually 1 to 2 years old.

The compensation committee should have procedures to ensure that the entire compensation process is thoroughly documented, whether for an initial contract or for a continuing agreement. This documentation should include "how the performance review was conducted (with the president's written self-review attached), how the comparative data were secured (also attached), and subsequent recommendations approved by the board. It should be made part of the chief financial officer's confidential files and made available for the institution's audit process" (Tranquada, 2001, p. 10). Compensation processes are discussed in more detail in chapters 4 and 5.

GOOD PRACTICES FOR COMPENSATING CEOS

In *The Compensation Committee*, Tranquada (2001) suggested that the committee should be prepared to answer 11 basic questions as it considers compensation for prospective presidents.

1. What do we need to provide in regard to compensation, benefits, and perquisites to acquire or retain an effective president?

2. Considering the entire budgetary situation, what is a responsible level of presidential compensation?

3. Where do we want to be in relation to our peers in presidential compensation?

4. Should a salary increase have a merit or incentive bonus component?

5. Do we agree on the major college objectives and priorities?

6. Do we have sufficient evidence of progress or lack thereof on each objective? (renewal contract)?

7. Have we looked at the objectives with respect to the amount of effort they require from the president?

8. What message do we want to deliver with the compensation recommendation?

9. Are we reasonably confident that our colleagues on the board will agree with our recommendation?

10. How will we communicate our recommendation to the full board?

11. How will our decision be communicated to outside constituencies? How will they respond to our decision?

PROS AND CONS

Just what are the advantages and disadvantages of a formal employment contract? The most obvious advantage to the president is confidence in the terms and conditions of his or her position. Often the board expects a new president to make changes, reorganize, meet accountability mandates, and take risks. When such changes are made, it is not uncommon for the president's popularity to suffer, particularly with long-term faculty and staff. Nielsen and Newton described a situation in which the trustees decided that their institution needed a major overhaul and hired a president who they believed could do the job:

> The new president understood his mandate to "sweep with a new broom" and went swiftly to work. The sweeping changes reached the media in no time, and the community began to look at the college with renewed scrutiny. In this instance, the board chose to disavow responsibility for the decisions made by the new president; the result was a barrage of criticism of the president that weakened his ability to lead. (1997, p. 34)

A well-drafted employment agreement can protect both the president and the institution from spur-of-the-moment decisions.

Furthermore, given the relatively short terms for many board members, the composition of the board may change. It is not unusual for an entirely new board to be in control 3 or 4 years after a new president is hired. That new board may not have the same commitment to the president that the hiring board had. In those circumstances, a complete and well-drafted employment agreement will have memorialized the expectations against which the president was expected to be evaluated and the nature of the ongoing relationships between the board and the president. Finally, a complete employment agreement will clearly spell out evaluation processes and delineate specific provisions for contract renewal and the conditions under which the president's employment would not be renewed or could be terminated.

That is not to say that every president is employed pursuant to the terms of a carefully crafted agreement. Sometimes a board may feel that a contract limits what it sees as its absolute power to dismiss the president, or it may believe that contracts have become too legalistic with a business mind-set that detracts from the collegial approach that has historically been the tradition of the academy. Some presidents agree. According to Jamienne S. Studley, former president of Skidmore College, "presidents' lawyers in some cases have become like agents for professional athletes, pushing for benefits far beyond what other employees at a college receive. 'It has the danger of distancing presidents from their campuses or creating a competition among presidents on the wrong sort of basis'" (cited in Basinger, 2002, p. A29). One president responding to the CCCS said, "I have been a president for almost forty years and have never had a contract."

While the arguments against having an employment agreement with the president continue to be made, the countervailing pressures continue to increase. As Kauffman (1980) suggested, presidents may be at the height of their earning power, but they have virtually no job security and no one to advocate for their well-being and advancement. In 1968, Ingraham discussed a similar theme. He lamented,

> The financial problems of the man without tenure, who has no house of his own, has many financial demands (greater than those incurred by others in the community) for the travel of his wife, for entertainment, for charity, and for a host of incidentals ... can be severe. Many suggest that the trustees be more systematic in reviewing the compensation of the president. (Ingraham, 1968, p. 153)

While some things have changed, much has remained the same in the intervening 40 years. Today we are more likely to lament the following needs in addition to base compensation: to find meaningful professional employment for a spouse; to meet technology needs such as laptops, cell phones, and PDAs; for deferred compensation and various forms of insurance; for child care; and for travel assistance for commuter marriages.

Responses to the CCCS supported the challenging financial issues that exist for some presidents and boards:

- The lack of contract and low pay make it very difficult for this system to attract candidates from other states.

- I'm a new president but have a sense that community college presidents are undercompensated compared to our university counterparts (taking into consideration size and enrollment of comparable institutions).

- Wage rates are modest in comparison to other organizations, particularly in light of the risk involved, hours required, and level of responsibility.

- Small community colleges are often in poor rural areas that cannot afford to provide the supplemental income and benefits of larger colleges. I feel some sort of standard benefits package should be recommended to all of our local boards of trustees.

- I think boards need to be more creative in determining benefits and consider moving their CEO closer to what exists in private sector organizations with a similar size budget and number of employees.

- It is hard for my board to set appropriate compensation in light of the economic situation of the tribal communities that we serve.

The lack of a well-crafted employment agreement may signal problems for the board and the president: "My contract is poorly written with the board generally unwilling to change it. It's also for only one year at a time. The board has had to buy out too many previous presidents, so I am paying per se for those sins. Ouch. I will be looking for a new presidency."

SUMMARY

A contract is nothing more than an agreement between two parties, through which each party exchanges benefits, duties, and obligations with the other. An employment contract is simply an agreement between the employer, in this case the board acting for the community college, and the employee, the president, through which each defines expectations, establishes obligations, and sets the ground rules for the ensuing relationship. The employment agreement should set forth the basic terms and conditions of employment, including, at a minimum, compensation, term of employment, benefits, processes and timelines for performance assessment, and the conditions and provisions for termination. Although the development of the contract is commonly the result of discussions between the board chair and the president, the complementary use of a compensation committee is an increasingly prevalent practice. Nevertheless, it is the full board that must ultimately exercise its legal authority in offering and amending written employment agreements.

Although some continue to argue against formal employment agreements, the advantages of a clear and specific statement of expectations of both parties in a carefully crafted employment agreement far outweigh the perceived disadvantages. A written employment contract serves as a vote of confidence on the part of the board in support of the president and gives the president the security that he or she needs to make difficult decisions in the best interests of the college. Finally, it is simply incorrect to say that in the absence of a written document there is no employment contract. A contract represents mutual understandings: Whether it is written or committed through a handshake simply indicates how easy or difficult it might be to determine the precise intentions of the parties. Above all, it must be remembered that an employment agreement is, in fact, a legal document. The president and the board may negotiate its operative terms, but its form and substance must be subject to the review and oversight of competent counsel.

3 Term of Appointment

"I HAVE PONDERED, FROM TIME to time, the quaint language found in almost all governing board bylaws and repeated in all letters of appointment received by new college and university presidents: 'The President shall serve at the pleasure of the Board.'" So begins chapter 1 of *At the Pleasure of the Board,* by Joseph Kauffman (1980). Just what is meant by the phrase, "pleasure of the board"? Kauffman continued, "How does one please or displease a board? Is not this status ambiguous for a chief executive, too vague to tolerate? How does it come to be that at the height of one's career effectiveness, one is placed in such a vulnerable situation? Most people work toward increasing job security. Why not a college president?" (p. 1).

WHAT THE PRESIDENTS SAY

The CCCS showed that many presidents still do work solely "at the pleasure of the board." In some cases, state law or tradition dictates the use of this phrase. For example, one president reported, "All presidents in the Alabama College System serve at the pleasure of the board.... We can be terminated by majority vote of the Board at any time." In Minnesota, "the 25 two year MnSCU [Minnesota State Colleges and Universities] president compensation packages are set by the Board of Trustees and managed by the Office of the Chancellor, Human Resources Department." A president in New York remarked, "I don't have a contract and neither do any other CUNY Presidents." In Virginia, "the Virginia Community College System office prepares the contracts for all 23 Virginia community college presidents. I think the contracts are pretty much the same (except for the salary)." In New Hampshire, a president reported, "at this point in time, the NH System does not use contracts of any type." Similarly, in Massachusetts, "multiple year contracts are not allowed by state law."

Sometimes confusion exists as to the reasons and justification for the lack of a separate formal employment agreement. In the survey, some presidents noted, "I don't know why we don't have contracts," and there is only an "informal agreement; the appointment is noted in Board minutes." One exasperated president commented, "While the board calls it a contract and it does contain my annual salary, it also explicitly states that I can be terminated at any time, for any reason, with no obligation to pay a salary beyond the date of termination, so I am not sure I would call it a contract." Presidents operating under such uncertain employment arrangements may face special challenges—and often a great deal of insecurity.

CONTRACT LENGTH

For those presidents who do work under a formal employment agreement, there are discernible patterns that have developed during the past decade as boards have paid more attention to the substance of these agreements. Vaughan and Weisman (1998) reported in their survey that the term of employment for community college presidents typically were either rolling (44%) or fixed (39%). Those presidents who did have employment contracts reported agreements of varying lengths. "Eighteen percent of the presidents with employment contracts have one-year contracts, 27 percent have three-year contracts, and 31 percent have contracts for four years" (Vaughan & Weisman, 1998, p. 65). Only 16% of presidents reported that they served at the will of the board.

The 2002 CCCS yielded percentages that were not greatly different from those in Vaughan and Weisman's 1998 survey, although there seemed to be a shift toward 3-year agreements. Of the 407 respondents to the 2002 survey, 19% had terms of 1 year, 12% had terms of 2 years, 49% had terms of 3 years, 13% had terms of 4 years, 5% had terms of 5 years, and 2% had indefinite terms. There were 70 nonresponses to the item.

The 2006 CCCS showed the trend toward longer contracts to be growing slowly, with 50% of the respondents indicating that they had 3-year contracts and 14% indicating that they had 4-year contracts—up just 1% from the previous survey. Of the 468 responding to this survey item, 19% indicated a term of 1 year, virtually unchanged from the previous survey 4 years ago. A term of 2 years was indicated by 10% of respondents, slightly down from the previous survey. Three-year terms were indicated by 50% of respondents, and 4-year terms were indicated by 14%. Other options respondents indicated were a 5-year term (6%), indefinite term (1%), and "other" (4%). Among the comments received from respondents were "four-year contract," "three-year rolling contract," "annual appointment letter," "two-year employment contract," "5-year contract," "six years," "general letter of appointment," and "annual contract." There were 80 nonresponses to this item. Some respondents indicated additional terms and arrangements for their contracts, ranging from 1 year renewable up to 3 years, to 2 ½ or 3 ½ years, to mutually renewable, to renewed every 3 years for a 5-year term. One respondent indicated "no specific terms addressed."

ADDITIONAL TERM COMPONENTS

Contract start dates also revealed some diversity, with the strong majority beginning, as would be expected, in July. However, every month of the year was represented at least once as a contract start date. With 247 of the 354 respondents to this item indicating a contract start date in July, a full 70% began at the traditional time; however, 8% had a start date in September, 6% in August, and 5% in January. Board history and preference, state law, county or other sponsoring agents' budget cycles, and the organization of the academic year all potentially affect contract start dates.

The presidents also reported a variety of rollover provisions. State law dictated some, but most were decided by board and CEO agreement. Of the 465 who responded to the item "Do you have a rolling agreement," 51% responded that they did have a rolling agreement, and 49% reported that they did not. Clearly, the rollover provision is more prevalent than it was a decade ago. The CCCS revealed a variety of rolling provisions, many of which were linked to performance:

- If performance review is good, an additional year is added. Three-year contract is ongoing, that is, currently it is for 2006–2009. In January it will be 2007–2010.

- 3-year rolling with annual extensions based on acceptable performance

- has been rolled forward each year for five years at board's discretion

- not automatic and is contingent on a positive evaluation

- Upon a satisfactory evaluation, one year is added to the contract. The maximum total length of contract, by law, is four years.

- currently rolling after two 5-year contracts

- Contract renews with approval during annual evaluation retreat.

One president indicated that the contract was "evergreen; annually renewed by one year … or NOT … so far (16 years) renewed out four years every year." Although there are many permutations of the rolling contract, it is well worth investigating in those states in which it is permissible. With a clearer future and time to make difficult decisions without a renewal date constantly looming, a president may be able to make more effective long-range decisions for the benefit and stability of the college.

Another possibility to consider in the initial contract is the "retreat" option, which enables the president to revert to a faculty (or sometimes other administrative) position if his or her tenure as president is terminated or expires. Where permissible by state and local laws and customs, a candidate may seek to negotiate faculty tenure and retreat rights as a part of the term of appointment. Thus, if at some point in the presidency the president loses the confidence of the board, he or she has the right to a faculty or other administrative position. One president responding to the CCCS commented, "[I was] hired as a full professor with tenure and released to be president and can return to the faculty." Although less common in community colleges than in 4-year colleges and universities, this option is becoming more acceptable, particularly in unionized environments. To the extent that they are negotiated, retreat rights and the consequences of reverting to a faculty position should be explicit. For example, will the salary be commensurate with the presidential salary or with a comparable faculty salary? What if there is no need for the president's academic specialty at the community college? How are rank and tenure to be decided, if these options exist at the college? Are there other available retreat options?

SUMMARY

The term of appointment varies greatly from college to college and state to state. Some states and systems impose limitations on the length of a contract. Some boards have had negative experiences with long-term contracts and are hesitant to offer anything other than year-to-year contracts. Annual contracts, although better than an entirely "at will" arrangement, do little to give a president the security needed to make sometimes unpopular but necessary decisions. The most common contract length is now 3 years. A rollover feature is increasingly used in contracts that essentially maintains the initial length of the contract as long as evaluations are positive and the board and CEO maintain mutual confidence. Boards may also want to consider a "retreat to faculty" option as part of a new or continuing contract. These types of continuing provisions send a powerful message to both the college community and the external community that the board fully supports the actions and authority of the president.

4 *Expectations and Evaluation*

ALTHOUGH IT MAY SEEM SURPRISING that so much is left to chance in the terms and conditions of employment, it is perhaps even more surprising that so little attention is paid to ongoing employment and the criteria or conditions for performance evaluation. As Gaskin (1997) has maintained, there is no single factor that is more important to the successful functioning of a community college than a mutually supportive relationship between a board of trustees and its president. That entails understanding the roles of each and accepting that there is a certain ambiguity and blending of roles. This type of focus provides value added to the organization and brings clarity to the CEO's role.

Furthermore, once a good match has been established between a board and a president, retention becomes an issue. It is difficult, time consuming, and disruptive to go through a presidential search with any frequency. Therefore, when things seem to be going well, the board needs to pay particular attention to doing what is necessary to retain a high-performing president. Evaluations should be handled with sensitivity, and the results should be shared in such a way as to motivate a president to continue to make tough decisions and do what is right for the institution, not just take the easy and popular way. The basis for evaluation should be a shared vision by the board and the president as well as compliance with the job description and the mission of the college (Nielsen & Newton, 1997, pp. 34, 35).

MORE SURVEY RESULTS

Responses to the CCCS showed that most presidents do have a board-conducted evaluation. In fact, of the 469 respondents to this survey item, 86% reported that they have a board-directed evaluation. Although most respondents (78%) were reviewed annually, 2% indicated that they had an evaluation "near the end of the contract period," 6% had "other" evaluation arrangements, and 14% said they had "no evaluation requirement." There were 79 nonresponses to this item.

Many of the presidents who do not have a board-conducted evaluation report to a chancellor who conducts the evaluation; others who are in a centralized system (they did not report to a board) are evaluated by the state president or the state commissioner. Other specific board-conducted evaluation requirements reported by CCCS respondents are as follows:

- two times per year

- every three years

- 5-year evaluation

- 6 months in the first year, annually afterward

- at the option of the board

- a formal evaluation is being explored for the first time

- annual self-evaluation and 3 year board evaluation

- one informal evaluation and one formal evaluation

Without a doubt, a clear set of expectations, goals, and standards of performance provides protection for both the president and the board. These standards should be mutually agreed on at the time of initial employment. There should be clearly stated times for assessment—usually annually. And most important, there should be established standards by which to assess the leadership of the president. "The president has a right to know by what criteria he or she will be judged. The trustees have an obligation to state in writing what those standards will be" (Nason, 1980, p. 77). Neff agreed that clear expectations are too often the missing piece in CEO–board relations: "A good statement of mutual expectations should focus the board and the president on the same issues. The statement also forms the basis of future evaluations" (1993, p. 20).

MUTUAL EXPECTATIONS

Just because an institution has a plethora of documents purporting to give guidance to a president, those documents do not necessarily target the specific expectations of the president. Nor do they necessarily indicate what the board wants to see accomplished. Mission statements, job descriptions, state regulations, institutional strategic plans, letters of intent to employ, and even contracts do not set forth the specific expectations for a president's tenure. A good statement of mutual expectations ought to accomplish several things. It should focus the board and the president on the same issues; deal with expectations in realistic terms including resources, priorities, and time lines; set forth goals in plain and detailed language; be agreed on and wholeheartedly supported by both the board and the president; improve communication between the board and the president; and serve as the basis for evaluation. In fact, "The board should evaluate the president's performance on the basis of clearly defined, mutually agreed on performance goals. The board should lead an annual presidential assessment process and provide feedback to the president that is both candid and constructive" (AGB, 2007, p. 9).

The CCCS was intended to establish what expectations were explicitly set out in an employment contract. The survey listed eight common CEO responsibilities, and respodents were asked whether the items were included in the written contract. The items were as follows:

1.   academic leadership

2.   community leadership

3.   fundraising responsibilities

4.   business and industry partnerships

5.   public school partnerships

6.   authority for hiring and firing

7.   communicating with the board

8.   performing a role with the board (secretary, treasurer, etc.)

As might be expected, academic leadership (56%) and community leadership (54%) were most frequently cited as being spelled out in the contract. Communicating with the board (52%), authority for hiring (48%), and business/industry partnerships (40%) were also highly visible in written contracts. Although a decade or so ago fundraising responsibilities were not seen as a high priority for community colleges, in the current survey 36% of respondents indicated that fundraising was included as a specific responsibility. Public school partnerships were listed in 29% of the contracts, and a particular function for the board (secretary, treasurer, etc.) was indicated as a part of the written contract by 19% of the respondents.

Many CEOs commented that although the responsibilities listed were indeed expectations, they were set forth either in a separate job description, board policy or bylaws, college personnel manual, or state statute. Examples include the following:

- Presidential duties are spelled out in board policy. The contract spells out salary, annual leave, other benefits.

- Though not in the contract, annual goals on partnerships and fundraising are set which are attached to a pay for performance system.

- Reference is made to state law and duties expected of the position.

- All duties required by law, by the policies of the board and by all applicable executive orders, federal, state, county, and bi-county rules and regulations.

- These are not specified in the contract: the contract cross-references the board bylaws with respect to duties of the president.

- All duties and responsibilities are spelled out in the job description and position announcement, which were referenced in the contract and attached but were not officially included in the body of the contract.

- The president is to be responsible for the overall management of the college including, but not limited to, all those duties incident to the office of president as set forth in the job description in the board policy manual and those obligations imposed.

Many respondents indicated that specific responsibilities were included as part of the contract language:

- organize and direct administrative and supervisory staff; make recommendations regarding building plans and location of ancillary support sites; aid in the preparation of all reports as required by the board; recommend rules, regulations, and policies

- oversee management of college property

- recommend operating and capital budgets; system wide planning; evaluation of campus presidents; oversight of collective bargaining with three faculty unions; establishment of system level committees, including a presidents' advisory council

- The contract addresses overall responsibility for advancing the mission and my full focus of time on those responsibilities.

- the chief executive officer and administrative officer of the college and the professional advisor to the board

- Long-range planning, formulating the budget, supervision of institutional building and grounds, student recruitment and services, faculty recruitment, implementation of actions to rectify issues that placed college on accreditation probation.

It is apparent from the comments of respondents that although general responsibilities and expectations are similar across college types, there are specific duties and tasks that are emphasized depending on the institution's perceived needs, the expectations of important constituencies, the level of centralization of the college or system, and past practices and traditions of the college and its governing board. Nevertheless, regardless of whether the responsibilities are set out in the contract or in a separate document, having specific expectations and goals delineated at the outset of a contract will help a president to focus limited time on the activities that are most important to the board.

> *Clear mutual expectations will not solve all the leadership problems of higher education. More explicitly stated, however, they might strengthen board–presidential working relations. They could make evaluations more effective for the board and the president, and ultimately, they could affect the ability of the institution to achieve its mission. (Neff, 1993, p. 23)*

THE ASSESSMENT PROCESS

Bornstein (1998) further considered the importance of systematic discussions on performance review and compensation. Although business leaders are often members of governing boards, they seem to apply different processes to rewarding a college president than they would apply to a business CEO. Perhaps that is because it is more difficult to evaluate the product. Bornstein stated,

> Education professionals traditionally are motivated more by the social value of what they do than by profits; thus, they generally are not compensated according to how many students or dollars they attract. As boards seek inducements to retain successful presidents, however, the business practice of providing "golden handcuffs" is becoming more common. (1998, p. 4)

Assessing the performance of the president is clearly the responsibility of the board. It is important that the responsibility be carried out with integrity, sensitivity, fairness, and dignity. Although presidents and boards may have shied away from formal evaluation practices in the past and relied on informal conversations, recent changes in federal law have prompted even those who have avoided such assessments to develop defensible practices. "In setting compensation levels, periodic benchmarking with peers is especially important, along with documentation of the practices used for the review of compensation and performance" (Ingram & Weary, 2000, p. 7). AGB further emphasized the importance of benchmarking, stating that "the board should base a president's compensation on explicit and justifiable benchmarks from within and outside the institution as well as on the marketplace for chief executives. The board must remain sensitive to the perceptions of stakeholders and the public" (AGB, 2007, p. 9).

Ingram and Weary also suggested that the annual assessment process should enable boards to respond to four important questions:

> (1) Do we really have a deep understanding of what our president does to lead and manage? (2) Do we really know how well the president is leading and managing? (3) Are the president's goal statements adequate and appropriate, and do we have ample opportunity to discuss and perhaps adjust them with the president? (4) Are we supporting the president in demonstrable ways, and are we genuinely interested in helping him or her grow professionally and personally? (Ingram & Weary, 2000, p. 14)

They went on to say that assessment should never be a game of "gotcha," nor should any one board member's personal agenda be allowed to dominate the evaluation process. The evaluation should not be used to discuss a singular negative event or single recent instance of perceived lack of judgment, nor should it be a time for the board to decide whether or not a president should move on.

If the president has lost the confidence of the board, that should be apparent to both parties and should be addressed in a timely way separate from the annual review process. In fact, in most cases it is desirable for the review process to be separate from the compensation process. The review process should be held before the compensation process, and the review process obviously informs the compensation process, but they should not be seen as one and the same. There may be, for example, times when a president has performed in an exemplary fashion, but budget restrictions prevent the board from substantially increasing compensation, despite the fact that goals have been met and even exceeded.

ASSESSMENT CRITERIA

The CCCS elicited the specific criteria that a board uses for evaluating a president, in addition to the general responsibilities and expectations of a CEO. As might be expected, great variation existed in the establishment of goals, the level of specificity of assessment criteria, and assessment of achievement. Some referred to formal processes defined by state statutes or state board policy: "evaluation instrument in state board policy"; "some items in the evaluation required by the state"; "duties and responsibilities as described in Florida law"; "areas specified in North Carolina state policy"; "an independent evaluator will perform an evaluation of my presidency at the end of five years of employment using the policies of the state board of governors."

More comments, however, were tied to specific local goals and objectives, usually mutually defined by the CEO and the board:

- The board and I agree on annual deliverables relative to our strategic plan, financial stability, accreditation, community/tribal relationships.

- It's a multi-page document. In a nutshell it covers communication, community service, finance, academic programming, enrollment, facilities, revenue enhancement and fund-raising.

- based on attainment of annual performance objectives

- enrollment, retention, diversity, economic development activities

- progress on the strategic plan, development of partnerships with the private sector, resource development, growing the college foundation endowment

- increase enrollment, increase retention percentages, increase graduation rates, community relations, active support of system office objectives, maintain college financial reserves

- personal attributes; relationships with trustees, students, faculty, business, government, community and educational groups; general administration and leadership in implementation of board policy, personnel administration, employee selection, leadership development

- represents college positively to community and academic leaders, promotes meaningful partnerships, promotes collaborative relationships with government and agencies, promotes learning-centered approach, manages change in inclusive ways

Clearly, these positions are demanding, and expectations for presidential leadership are very high. It is important for boards and presidents to agree on the prioritization of goals and objectives, because even the brightest and most ambitious presidential star cannot possibly accomplish all goals at a uniformly high level.

Ingram and Weary (2000) proposed that a president and board use what they described as "The Chief Executive's Annual Management Review Statement" as the basis for the annual performance assessment. This assessment has three basic components: "retrospective," "prospective," and "other information." In the retrospective section, a president delineates the progress made toward last year's mutually agreed-upon goals. Personal and institutional achievements beyond the goals are also discussed. Particular disappointments or frustrations are detailed. Relationships with faculty, staff, and community and business leaders are discussed. Finally, any personal or family issues that have an impact on the presidency are brought to the board's attention.

The prospective component details the challenges and opportunities that the president sees ahead. The president lists 5 to 10 primary goals for the institution over the next year and beyond and includes any other thoughts, ambitions, or ideas that might not have been discussed in other sections of the report. The "other information" component gives the CEO an opportunity to present any problems, including financial and morale issues, that might help the board assess the college's health and progress. The Management Review Statement forms the basis for assessment, provides an opportunity for discussion of the direction of the college, and links to future compensation decisions. For an in-depth discussion of options for assessment of the president, as well as of the board, Ingram and Weary's (2000) *Presidential and Board Assessment in Higher Education* is an excellent resource.

SUMMARY

Evaluations are an important component of the board–CEO relationship. Both new and continuing presidents need to know exactly what the board expects to be accomplished, the resources available, and the time line for completion. The format and time lines for an assessment of those expectations should be part of an annual goal-setting and review process. The way in which a board intends to evaluate the effectiveness of the CEO should be spelled out clearly in an initial contract and reviewed and modified, if necessary, annually. Compensation and extension of contract provisions are tied inevitably to performance evaluation; however, where possible, those processes should be carried out separately so that full attention can be devoted to each. Having a full understanding of their mutual roles and responsibilities will permit a board and president to carry out their complementary roles in a way that ultimately allows the college to move forward with a focus on fulfilling its mission.

5 *Compensation*

ALTHOUGH IT IS CERTAINLY TRUE that a person does not aspire to a college presidency to become rich, it is a fallacy to assume that candidates are indifferent to financial considerations.

> *In the end, say economists, it is about money, not just about "principle." What we earn—and the process by which we are paid—matters. It matters to the long-term viability of organizations that they are able to attract and retain the most capable and talented leaders in their profession. And it matters to those who hold top leadership positions that they feel appreciated and that their exemplary work is rewarded financially and in other ways. (Atwell & Wellman, 2000, p. v)*

Upon the successful completion of a search process, the negotiating of terms and conditions of employment, including benefits and compensation, must be undertaken. Similarly, following the evaluation of a president, compensation issues need to be addressed. Compensation, including benefits and the process by which raises will be determined, is usually determined by the board chair and executive committee of the board of trustees or by a special compensation committee of the board. This chapter addresses compensation and raises, bonuses and incentive pay, outside employment, foundation supplements, and retirement income.

COMPENSATION AND RAISES

It is the responsibility of the board chair to provide leadership in devising a contract with a competitive and reasonable compensation package. Most CEOs surveyed indicated that their base compensation is stated in their employment contract. Whereas 91% indicated that the salary was a part of the contract, only 9% stated that the compensation did not appear as part of the written contract.

Boards should reward their CEOs fairly and generously for their efforts. "Presidents should not have to plead for adequate compensation or negotiate for themselves. Boards that take the initiative on such matters send a clear signal that they value their chief executives and that presidential time and energy are best spent on the complex responsibilities of leadership" (Bornstein, 1998, p. 4).

Rewarding fairly can best be accomplished when governing boards have appropriate compensation policies and procedures in place. Although the governing board has the responsibility to attract and retain an effective president, it must do so in a way that is acceptable to its various constituencies. The process of providing competitive salary and benefits can best be understood when there is a formal process that requires "rationality, formality in process and record keeping, and an identifiable relationship with performance" (Ingram, 1997, p. 8).

In the CCCS, CEOs were asked to detail how raises are determined as part of a contractual agreement. Surprisingly, nearly two thirds (62%) of respondents indicated that their contract contained no written process for receiving raises. The survey also included several specific questions about the criteria for increases, whether or not those criteria were stipulated in the contract. The responses are shown in Table 1.

TABLE 1. CRITERIA FOR DETERMINING SALARY INCREASES

| | Yes | | No | |
Criterion	#	%	#	%
Meritorious service	167	30	381	70
Achievement of goals	178	32	370	68
State increases	186	34	362	66
Other employees' increases	192	35	356	65
Regular increments	59	11	489	89
Discretion of the board	327	60	221	40

Source: AACC (2006)

As Table 1 shows, the most frequently used method of determining salary increases for presidents is simply the discretion of the board. Meritorious service and achievement of goals at 30% and 32%, respectively, do not appear to be a major factor in determining salary increases. The findings from this survey indicate that the link between performance and salary increase is tenuous at best. Boards and presidents should spend a great deal of time and thought determining defensible standards that can be used to justify and explain salary increases. Raises are less subject to public criticism when the processes and criteria for providing a salary increase are clearly stated as part of the contract, are related to performance, and still ensure the appropriate discretion that is due a board, chancellor, or system president.

GOOD PRACTICES FOR COMPENSATING CEOS

In an article titled "Searching for Reason in Presidential Compensation," Ingram (1997) provided a useful checklist of good practices for executive compensation. Realizing that governing boards of colleges and universities are held to a higher standard than are boards of for-profit businesses and that tax-supported public institutions are held to a higher standard still, he suggested that boards protect themselves and their presidents by maintaining good practices.

- Boards should designate a compensation committee to review the existing compensation package on an annual basis.

- Boards should be clear that they relate compensation to performance by asking the president to prepare a self-evaluation that details the goals and objectives of the past year and progress and problems in achieving those goals and objectives. Part of the self-assessment should be developing a new and/or revised set of goals for the coming year. Simultaneously, the board should gather reliable information about the compensation packages of peer institutions to use as comparative data in deciding salary and benefits adjustments.

- Boards should document the oversight and decision-making processes of the compensation committee. The entire board should be on record as supporting the action of the committee.

SALARY BONUSES AND INCENTIVE PAY

Salary bonuses, most often associated with the corporate world, are not common in higher education. A salary bonus is usually linked to a particular goal, such as enrollment or fundraising. Less often, a signing bonus may be offered. In the CCCS, only 2% of the CEOs indicated that they received a signing bonus. Sometimes a salary bonus may be linked to longevity and retention and may be another type of golden handcuff to ensure continued service of a valued president. The CCCS indicated that 12% of respondents were offered some type of retention bonus. The criteria for retention bonuses varied widely and seemed to be limited only by the creativity of the board and applicable laws, as this sample of responses shows:

- an incentive of $15,000 after three years

- 20% of salary per year after retirement

- additional life insurance

- yearly annuity

- 5% of salary when retiring

- bonuses go up for each year that I stay

- received a $10,000/year retention bonus

- 12 months' salary for over 12 years service

- at five years I get 10% of ending salary

- after 3rd year, bonuses for each year

- annual retention incentive $7,500

- golden handcuff equal to 20% of annual salary

- longevity after seven years

- $15,000 TSA for completion of 3 years

Bonuses for the purpose of retention or reward are becoming more acceptable in community colleges, but not all constituencies see them as appropriate.

Some believe bonuses for college and university presidents are inappropriate or politically unseemly and argue against bonus arrangements on that basis. Others believe they offer appropriate incentives for the achievement of goals. A benefit of a bonus system is that it requires the board and president to discuss goals and quantifiable performance measures. (Atwell & Wellman, 2000, p. 51)

Opportunities for bonus pay do not appear to be numerous on the basis of the CCCS: Only 21% of the respondents indicated that they were eligible for some type of bonus pay other than a signing bonus or a retention bonus. A concern expressed by some CEOs was that bonuses are not part of the base, which means that retirement contributions are not paid on these amounts.

Those who were eligible for bonuses were asked to indicate which performance measures determined their bonuses. Table 2 summarizes those responses. The responses clearly indicate that some boards rely on more than one measure to determine bonus pay; however, board evaluation is the most frequently cited criterion for a bonus, followed by the achievement of specifically stated goals and exemplary or meritorious service beyond what is expected. Comments from respondents about the basis for performance bonuses included the following:

- 10% per year, paid every 2 years, if goals are met

- based on certain goals/objectives accomplished

- general bonus based on evaluation

- successful SACS reaffirmation

- satisfactory performance

- college meeting or exceeding state performance measures

- employee satisfaction measures; partnerships with business, government, etc.

TABLE 2. PERFORMANCE MEASURES USED TO DETERMINE BONUSES

Performance Measure	#	%
Bonuses are not based on performance	20	17
Endowment/fundraising	19	16
Financial performance (e.g., cost containment)	23	20
Enrollment increases	26	22
Student success measures	24	21
Achievement of other specifically stated goals	38	33
Exemplary or meritorious service	34	29
Board evaluation	45	39
Peer college review	4	3

Source: AACC (2006)

LIMITS ON OUTSIDE EMPLOYMENT

Many times presidents have invitations to engage in consulting, paid scholarly work, or paid board service. They may have opportunities to receive honoraria for delivering keynote addresses or making other presentations. Boards and CEOs need to determine at the outset, during the negotiation of the initial contract, what the limits of such outside employment will be. Some boards believe that the CEO must give complete time and effort to the position of the presidency and that no outside income is allowed. Other boards may see value to the institution through a president's outside presentations and service on boards. Boards may elect to set a specific number of days that a president may be absent for the purpose of consulting or other paid outside employment. Alternatively, boards may require that a president take vacation days for any such paid activities. Outside employment is one of the areas in which misunderstandings can occur if such provisions are not made clear at the beginning of employment.

Of the 548 CEOs who responded to the question concerning restrictions on outside employment, 55% indicated no restrictions, and 45% indicated restrictions of some type. Some indicated that state law limited the number of days, or the amount of compensation, or both, that could be earned; others listed board restrictions such as 3 days, 10 days, and 12 days. Many presidents reported that there was an understanding about outside employment, but it was not delineated in the contract. Comments such as "not addressed in any way," "it's never come up," "hasn't been discussed," "not addressed in my contract," and "not in contract, no verbal restrictions" were common. Some indicated an outright ban on all outside earnings with explanations such as "strictly prohibited by state ethics code," "not permitted," "no outside employment allowed," "none permitted by state law," and "devote full and exclusive time and attention as president." Many required prior approval by the board or the chancellor.

Outside earnings were restricted by the number of days per year by only 8% of the respondents: "8 hours per week"; "allowed 7 days for consulting"; "if more than 3 days, notify board chair." Nearly 35% of respondents indicated that outside earnings were restricted by the requirement to take vacation days. "Required to take vacation, but also notify the state personnel office." Just over 1% indicated that the amount of money they were allowed to earn was stipulated. In fact, of those who responded concerning compensation for activities outside regular responsibilities as college president, the amounts were relatively small in comparison with salaries and other benefits. The average earnings for consulting services were approximately $2,500; the average earnings for paid board service were $2,700; the average earnings for honoraria for speeches and presentations were $1,300; and other outside compensation averaged $660.

Presidents seem to be aware of the potential for negative reactions from engaging in paid outside activities. Comments such as "I donate all outside earnings to the college scholarship foundation" and "I generally donate honoraria to the college foundation" were typical. The survey showed that presidents also realize the importance of keeping the board well informed about any outside activities through comments such as "all activities are subject to approval by board of trustees," "must have board approval for any outside employment," "I'm not really required to but feel I need to," and "in consultation with the board chair and with the understanding that activities not interfere with the president's normal duties and effectiveness."

SUPPLEMENTS FROM PUBLIC INSTITUTION FOUNDATIONS

It is relatively common for institutions with associated foundations to use foundation funds to improve the salary and benefits of the president. Although in most cases it is legal to supplement the president's salary from foundation funds, it may not be politically wise from a public relations and alumni point of view. Atwell and Wellman (2000) suggested that rather than use foundation funds to supplement salary, it may be more appropriate to use foundation funds to support the office of the presidency through providing entertainment expenses, club memberships, spousal travel, and other benefits that are not directly related to salary.

RETIREMENT BENEFITS

A wide variety of retirement benefits are possible, limited only by the willingness of the board, the rules and regulations of the governing entity, and state and federal laws. In the CCCS, presidents were asked to indicate what types of retirement benefits they received. More than half (58%) indicated that they participated in a defined benefit or traditional pension plan, usually sponsored by the state. More than two thirds of respondents (68%) indicated that they participated in a defined contribution plan. The numbers reflect that some CEOs participated in both defined benefit and defined contribution plans. Only 15% of the respondents indicated that they participated in an additional supplemental executive retirement plan.

Other types of retirement benefits were diverse and linked to the culture and capabilities of the college. Examples include the following:

- college-owned annuity

- 457b

- state retirement system

- life insurance plan

- 49% workload retirement for 5 years

- purchase of out-of-state service

- help with health insurance based on years of service

- TIAA-CREF contributions

- long-term care for CEO and spouse (life)

Postretirement benefits can be very important to CEOs who are nearing the end of their active careers. Such benefits can often be negotiated at the time of an initial contract or after a particularly successful evaluation when the board is seeking ways other than direct compensation to retain a high-performing president. Perhaps the most common benefit is the continuation of health insurance following retirement for a set period of time or throughout the lifetime of the president. The CCCS revealed that 37% of the CEOs had the benefit of a continued health insurance plan, whereas 63% did not have the benefit.

As a way of retaining a president, some boards may elect to build a tiered system: If a president retires in 5 years, for example, the board will pay 50% of premium costs for postretirement health insurance. If the president retires in 10 years, the board will pay 100% of health insurance premiums for the lifetime of the president. The board, where permitted by law, may also extend health and other benefits to the CEO's spouse after the CEO's retirement. These types of benefits are often referred to as golden handcuffs because they function to keep a high-performing president at the institution by offering attractive financial benefits for doing so.

Despite the obvious benefits, deferred compensation is not a benefit frequently cited in community college president's contracts. Only 30% of those responding to the question in the CCCS reported that deferred compensation was offered, whereas 70% indicated that it was not offered. Where possible, the provision of some type of deferred compensation is a great benefit to a president and indicates a progressive and informed board that is willing to offer long-term benefits to a potential or continuing president. These benefits can be complex and have significant tax implications; therefore, it is imperative that experienced legal counsel be involved in preparing and reviewing deferred compensation benefits.

SUMMARY

Every employment contract inherently deals with compensation. In addition to base compensation, however, an employment agreement should also detail the process for receiving raises and bonuses. Boards may have very differing ideas of the appropriateness of presidents engaging in outside employment such as paid speaking engagements or paid service on boards; these expectations should be delineated. If a college intends to use supplements from a college foundation for salary or benefits for the president, the appropriate use of those funds should be spelled out in the contract. Of great interest and benefit to CEOs is the provision of a variety of retirement benefits, including deferred compensation. Thoughtful boards will discuss all the financial options concerning appropriate retirement benefits legally available to them to support and retain a high-performing CEO. Inasmuch as tax laws and state and federal laws are constantly changing in this area, it is critically important to develop these contract components with the assistance of a qualified attorney.

6 *Standard Benefits*

STANDARD BENEFITS ARE THOSE THAT are extended to most full-time employees, as well as benefits that are most frequently cited as part of a CEO's compensation package. Standard benefits include insurance benefits such as health, life, accidental death and dismemberment (AD&D), disability, and long-term care insurance; leave policies such as vacation, sick, disability, travel, and sabbatical leaves; use of a college-purchased, leased, or subsidized car; moving and relocation expenses; and professional development. Those benefits that are more uniquely tailored to the specific needs and responsibilities of a particular CEO and are distinct from most other employee benefits are categorized as enhanced benefits and will be discussed in chapter 7.

INSURANCE BENEFITS

Although there is an array of possible insurance benefits that a board can provide, this section reviews some of the most common that might be extended to a CEO and, under some circumstances, to dependents.

Health Insurance

Health insurance benefits, including medical, prescription drug, dental, hearing, and vision, are standard for nearly every full-time employee. In addition to making these benefits available to a president, a board should use every avenue permitted by law to pay the attached premiums. In most cases, these benefits can also be extended to family members. Again, wherever possible, the board can make a more attractive package by agreeing to pick up the costs for basic family health, dental, and vision insurance.

The CCCS reflected the almost universal availability of these insurance benefits; however, in many instances, they are a part of the standard benefits for all employees and as such are not a part of the CEO contract. Instead, they are referenced in board policy or in an employee handbook. The following tables provide responses to questions about medical, prescription drug, dental, hearing, and vision insurance for the CEO (Table 3) and for dependents (Table 4). The possible responses were "offered and paid 100%," "offered and paid partially," "offered but not paid," and "not offered." Respondents were also asked whether or not the benefit was written into the contract.

TABLE 3. HEALTH INSURANCE BENEFITS OFFERED TO CEOS

Benefit	Paid #	Paid %	Part paid #	Part paid %	Not paid #	Not paid %	Not offered #	Not offered %	In contract #	In contract %
Medical	289	53	234	42	12	2	8	2	88	16
Prescription	183	33	298	54	18	3	26	5	76	14
Dental	179	33	241	44	82	15	23	4	75	14
Hearing	90	16	129	24	43	8	160	29	28	5
Vision	136	25	195	36	78	14	81	15	49	9

Note. Percentages may not equal 100% as a result of rounding.

Source: AACC (2006)

TABLE 4. HEALTH INSURANCE BENEFITS OFFERED TO CEOS' DEPENDENTS

Benefit	Paid #	Paid %	Part paid #	Part paid %	Not paid #	Not paid %	Not offered #	Not offered %	In contract #	In contract %
Medical	139	25	246	45	90	16	33	6	61	11
Prescription	100	18	269	49	89	16	45	8	55	10
Dental	108	20	215	39	127	23	46	8	53	10
Hearing	52	10	126	23	62	11	160	29	25	5
Vision	82	15	180	33	95	17	104	19	34	6

Note. Percentages may not equal 100% as a result of rounding.

Source: AACC (2006)

Annual Physical Exam

Often a board will want to include a provision for an annual comprehensive physical exam, assuring the board that the president is indeed fit to perform the necessary duties. Costs for a basic physical exam are usually covered by health insurance policies; however, a comprehensive exam with a variety of tests may not be. Therefore, generally the contract agreement stipulates that the president will be reimbursed for costs not covered by medical insurance. Comments from CEOs included "annual physical examination report required to be submitted to the board," "must have annual physical exam," and "college covers any cost not covered under medical for an annual physical."

Life, Accidental Death and Dismemberment, and Disability Insurance

Life insurance is very affordable when purchased for a group. Depending on the president's family situation, additional life insurance may be the difference between a reasonable lifestyle and poverty for the family should the president die while in office. Many presidents have requested that the college provide coverage of 2.5 times the annual salary. This seems to be an industry standard (Cotton, 2002). In addition, many boards provide AD&D insurance as well as traditional life insurance.

Disability insurance is often relegated to a lower priority. However, it is relatively inexpensive, and it is absolutely vital in the event of an accident or illness that keeps a CEO away from work. In discussing disability benefits, Cotton indicated that everyone in higher education should have a disability policy that covers at least 60% of current salary. However, many colleges have policies that cap disability payments at a low level. Although such policies may cover 60% of an employee's salary, they often have a benefit cap of as low as $5,000 per month.

> *Assuming a president earns a salary of $200,000 a year, 60% of that amount would be [$]120,000. If a college has a disability insurance policy with a $5,000 a month benefit cap on it, only 30% of the president's salary would be forthcoming in the event he or she became totally disabled while working for the college. Unless a president has significant other assets, or resources, I view that level of coverage as insufficient to adequately protect the president and his or her family in the event of a catastrophe. In cases like this, the president ought to bring this inequity to the attention of the board chairman or the compensation committee and request additional disability coverage to bring the level to 60% of base salary. Specific add-on policies are available in the marketplace. (Cotton, 2002)*

The CCCS showed that a majority of CEOs (57%) receive personal life insurance as a wholly paid benefit, whereas fewer (35%) receive short-term disability insurance as a wholly paid benefit. Dependent life insurance is usually available but not paid. Table 5 shows responses to questions about life, AD&D, and disability insurance as well as life insurance for dependents.

TABLE 5. OTHER INSURANCE BENEFITS OFFERED TO CEOS AND DEPENDENTS

Benefit	Paid #	Paid %	Part paid #	Part paid %	Not paid #	Not paid %	Not offered #	Not offered %	In contract #	In contract %
CEO life	312	57	147	27	45	8	23	4	80	15
CEO AD&D	172	31	82	15	115	21	101	18	40	7
CEO disability	194	35	91	17	107	20	81	15	52	10
Dependent life	26	5	52	10	127	23	203	37	17	3

Note. Percentages may not equal 100% as a result of rounding.

Source: AACC (2006)

Long-Term Care Insurance

A relatively new type of insurance, long-term care insurance is a benefit that CEOs and boards may well consider. Cotton described this insurance, which is intended to fill in gaps in employer-sponsored health insurance plans and Medicare, as follows:

> *A long-term-care insurance policy provides reimbursement for custodial-care expenses (i.e., home health care or nursing home care) not covered by health insurance or disability income policies. In the event of a disability while working, these policies can provide the money to pay for custodial-care expenses and ensure that assets accumulated for retirement are not consumed prematurely. In addition, although disability benefits typically end at retirement, long-term care insurance policies can provide benefits on a postretirement basis. Since long-term care insurance policies are considered health insurance policies, they receive very favorable tax treatment; premiums and benefits are not subject to current or future taxation. Also this is one of the few fringe benefits that may be provided to spouses. Finally, providing the president and*

spouse with a long-term care insurance policy may be another opportunity to use "golden handcuffs." The board of trustees may opt to structure this portable benefit to be paid up in 10 years or at retirement. (Cotton, 2002)

In surveying the availability of this benefit, it was somewhat surprising to see the frequency with which it was considered, perhaps indicating increasing sophistication on the part of the board and the CEO—as well as the aging of presidents! Nearly 30% of respondents had long-term care insurance either wholly paid (17%) or partially paid (12%). Another 24% of respondents indicated that long-term care insurance was offered but not paid for by the college; 27% indicated that long-term care insurance was not offered. Interestingly, only 6% of CEOs indicated that long-term care insurance was specifically included in the written employment agreement.

LEAVE POLICIES

Leave policies vary greatly among institutions and are frequently governed by state law or system regulations. Most often, leave policies are similar for all categories of employees, with allowances for time in service. This section presents descriptions of vacation, sick, disability, and sabbatical leave.

Vacation Leave

According to Vaughan and Weisman's 1998 study, presidents earned an average of 22 days of annual or vacation leave each year, which is essentially the same amount they earned in 1984. In most cases, unused annual leave is simply lost; it does not transfer into cash compensation. Responses to the 2002 CCCS showed a variety of arrangements for vacation days; however, the most frequently cited number was 20, followed closely by 24 (AACC, 2002). Thus, it appeared that most presidents were eligible for 4 to 5 weeks of vacation time per year. Responses to the 2006 CCCS were similar, with an average of 22.3 vacation days, excluding holidays. Nearly three quarters of the presidents surveyed also indicated that they received an average of 5 personal leave days that could be used as they saw fit. The number of vacation days has remained fairly constant for the past 20 years (AACC, 2006).

Sick Leave

Sick leave is usually granted at the same level as that provided for other employees. Depending on state and local regulations, sick leave may be accumulated. Unused leave may be compensated at the termination of employment or after the accumulation of a certain number of days. Some colleges have policies covering donated leave, and presidents may feel pressure to donate unused leave in the event of the extended illness of staff or faculty. The contract should clearly spell out the conditions concerning sick leave or refer to college policy. Respondents to the CCCS indicated that they earned an average of 16 days of sick leave per year.

Disability Leave

The extended disability of a president not only creates hardships for the president and family, but also it creates instability and uncertainty for the college. Some contracts state specifically the time period in which a president can be absent from the full-time responsibilities of the job before it would be necessary for him or her to leave employment and allow the college to seek new leadership. There should be specific provisions in the contract, including a physician's professional assessment of the nature and duration of the illness or accident, a timetable for recovery, and alternatives including special assignment, appointment of an interim president, types of leaves available, and the extent of leave before termination. Any contractual requirements must be in accordance with applicable state and federal laws (ADA, FMLA, etc.) that may provide additional insights and definitions of disability.

Sabbatical Leave

Sabbatical leaves, although not the norm in community colleges, are becoming more common, particularly in unionized environments in which faculty have negotiated sabbatical rights into employment agreements. A sabbatical leave can be a useful tool in retaining an effective president. In the CCCS, of the 543 respondents who answered the question, "As president, are you eligible for sabbatical leave?", 32% responded that they were eligible, and 68% indicated that they were not. Comments on the length and conditions of the sabbatical, when granted, were as varied as the institutions.

- one semester at full pay or two semesters at half pay, sabbatical may be taken after seven years of full time employment

- one semester at full pay every 4th year

- one year full pay taken during last year of employment

- 3 months every five years

- eligible after five years of employment, at 50% pay for up to one year

- 6 months at 75% pay

- 2 months paid administrative leave every five years

- time and pay is at the discretion of the chancellor—individuals are eligible at any time

- 4 months at full pay; up to 12 months at 60% pay

- after 10 years of employment up to one year

- one semester at full pay but I am not likely to ever apply for this—too busy

It may be that a board could consider providing an extended leave—a month or two—as a more politically acceptable compromise, rather than the traditional semester-length sabbatical. The opportunity to recharge, read, travel, teach, or write can be very invigorating to a leader who has had little opportunity to pursue any other interests while serving as CEO. In a healthy and well-functioning organization, it is quite possible to appoint a short-term acting president while the CEO is on sabbatical. The prospect of a sabbatical leave may be a useful retention incentive and provide a unique professional development opportunity to a valued leader.

TRAVEL EXPENSE ALLOWANCE

Most boards reimburse the president for all expenses related to official business travel. However, the limits of that travel may need to be indicated in the contract. May the president fly first or business class and be reimbursed, or is it more appropriate to travel coach? Is there a set mileage reimbursement for the use of personal vehicles? Is the president to be provided a college credit card to charge all expenses, or should the president retain receipts from expenditures and be reimbursed?

Another sensitive issue that should be dealt with in the initial contract is spousal travel. Many boards will reimburse the travel expenses of a spouse who accompanies a president to a professional meeting. Other boards may believe that paying for spousal travel gives the public appearance of a junket and may decline to pay any such expenses. Comments from presidents concerning spousal travel indicated that when provisions were made for spouses, they were rather limited: "may accompany president at college expense for selected functions"; "no airfares, but reasonable costs associated with registration, meals"; "spouse may accompany me on professional trips"; "registration for events requiring spouse attendance"; "$1,000 travel to conferences." To avoid misunderstanding and embarrassment for the president and the institution, policies on spousal travel need to be clearly delineated.

Recognizing that professional travel is an important part of the CEO's responsibilities, some boards provide travel accident insurance. In the CCCS, CEOs were asked whether travel accident insurance were provided and, if so, whether the insurance fully or partly paid for. Of 548 respondents, 13% indicated that the insurance was provided and fully paid, 5% indicated that the insurance was offered and partly paid, 12% indicated that the insurance was offered but not paid, and 45% indicated that travel accident insurance was not offered. Less than 3% of respondents indicated that travel accident insurance was written into the contract.

CAR OR CAR ALLOWANCE

Many institutions provide the president with a car. The board should clearly state the appropriate use of the car. For example, some boards may specify that the car is for business use only. In that case, the vehicle is to be used only to get to and from work, to conferences and business meetings, and to transport college guests. Some boards indicate that the car is for the president's business and personal use. CEOs who are permitted personal use of the car need to be careful to record the various uses of the car, because the value of the personal use may be considered taxable income. One president responding to the CCCS commented that the "contract specifies that I have 'continuous' use of the car that the college provides, i.e., for personal as well as professional use, and the college provides for all upkeep, maintenance and insurance costs." Other CEOs indicated that the car was used as a type of reward, that is, they were able to keep the car after a certain number of years of service or upon retirement.

Responsibilities for maintenance and insurance of the car should be explicitly stated. Unless the vehicle is owned by the president, it will be insured through the institution. The college's risk management officer should be involved in determining the parameters of the applicable insurance, including who may be permitted to operate the vehicle other than the president.

Responses to the CCCS confirmed that assistance with car expenses was an expectation that was usually met either through a college-provided car (purchased or leased) or an expense allowance for the business use of a personal vehicle. Of the 536 responding to the question on car use, 18% indicated that they did not have a college car or car allowance, whereas 82% indicated that they did have access to a college car. Interestingly, 20% of those with a car or car allowance did not have rules, regulations, or conditions of use as part of the written employment contract. CEOs and boards would be well advised to include the conditions of use of a college-owned or leased car as part of the formal contract.

MOVING AND RELOCATION EXPENSES

Relocation expenses are frequently part of the initial package to make it easier for a CEO to move to a new area. Relocation may include reimbursement for several visits to the area and at least one visit that includes family. Other expenses, including short-term home or apartment rental, house hunting, and car rentals, may need to be initiated, depending on the circumstances. Inasmuch as moving—especially long-distance moving of a large household—can be expensive, it is important that conditions be explicitly stated. The board may be willing to stipulate a dollar amount that will be paid—for example, moving expenses not to exceed $8,000. A more attractive option for the CEO is for the board to agree to cover all moving expenses, regardless of cost, because those costs are often uncertain beforehand. There should be clarity also as to whether moving expenses include professional packing and unpacking or actual transportation costs only. Is the board willing to pay the costs of a professional mover, or is the president expected to engage a do-it-yourself company such as U-Haul?

Less frequently addressed, but of great value to an outgoing CEO, is the board's agreement to pay relocation expenses at the end of the presidency, if certain conditions are met. For example, the president must be at the end of the contract term or be terminated without cause. One president indicated that "upon retirement (after at least 5 years of service), moving expenses are paid to any location in the continental U.S." This type of benefit is best negotiated as part of the initial contract; it is much harder to negotiate such an agreement well into the presidency.

PROFESSIONAL DEVELOPMENT AND RENEWAL

It is not accurate to assume that once a president secures a position he or she has no further need for professional growth and development. In fact, just the opposite is more likely the case. Once a president gauges the extensive demands of the position, which probably are not fully understood until at least 6 months into a new presidency, there will undoubtedly be a realization of the need for further professional development to meet the challenges of an increasingly complex role. Of course, professional development needs are highly personal and dependent on the CEO's level of experience, education, and time on the job.

In a study of professional development needs of presidents in North Carolina, South Carolina, and Georgia (Wallin, 2002), presidents consistently indicated that their chief barriers to further professional development were time and funding. The presidents were asked to rank the types of professional development that were most useful to them in improving their effectiveness. National conferences, state and regional conferences, and statewide presidents' meetings consistently ranked above formal leadership programs. Presidents seem to learn a great deal from the opportunity to discuss issues, problems, and solutions with their CEO colleagues. However, the most frequently mentioned activity that presidents believed would make them more effective was the opportunity for some type of sabbatical leave. The options and benefits to providing a sabbatical leave were discussed previously. At the very least, a board should be attentive to professional development needs of the president and be sure that time and resources are provided not only to allow but also to encourage a president to engage in growth activities.

Comments from CCCS respondents indicated that, for the most part, boards were aware and supportive of professional development for their CEOs. Many simply indicated that although no contract provision exists for professional development, it is expected and compensated:

- no incentives expressly provided or written in—however, I may choose to attend and the expenses will be paid

- professional development is available; no incentives to participate, but paid for

- no monetary incentives, but it is anticipated and expected that I am to be current in field

- monies to attend workshops/conferences; not written in contract

- unlimited

- College budget allows for participation in professional development. They are not written into the contract.

- College pays for professional development. Incentives are not written into the agreement.

- strong encouragement and all expenses paid; not written into contract

- I can essentially attend any professional development activity I choose, fully paid. There is no contract language to support this.

Other comments indicate more specificity from the board or that professional development expectations are written into the contract or both:

- cover costs for Harvard Institute for New Presidents, possibly others on request

- I am allowed to participate in professional development within reason; no more than twice per semester unless approved by the BOT.

- required to engage in professional development, at my expense

- expectation and funding to actively serve as a member of the Board of Directors of the League for Innovation in the Community College and to attend national conferences, AACC, ACCT, etc.

- in contract that college will pay for my professional development; amount and nature of professional development not addressed

- tuition waivers

- Professional development is expected by the board and included in the contract; travel and registration fees for these activities are covered and specified in the contract.

- college pays—AACC and ACCT are written into contract

- 10 days per year for professional development

- The contract says all such reasonable expenses will be paid with no specific details.

- $2,500 annual in contract

- I have a $3,000/year professional budget; contract language establishes an expectation that I will seek professional development opportunities.

- three national conferences per fiscal year

- strong support for institutes and travel; major conferences and consulting and writing

- President is provided 5 days per year for professional writing.

- full support for conference travel, professional organization memberships

- reimbursement for attendance at meetings written in contract, no limit stated

- I can participate in any domestic professional development I believe is appropriate, and in international travel after discussion and approval by the board.

SUMMARY

Every employment agreement deals with compensation, and almost all include benefits. Certain benefits, such as health and life insurance, are fairly standard. Boards can assist CEOs by providing for the institution to pay all or part of the premium costs and including dependent coverage where appropriate. Leaves, too, are relatively uniform for all professional employees, depending on length of service. Boards might consider additional vacation or personal leave as well as some form of sabbatical leave for the benefit of the CEO where permitted by state and local rules and regulations. The appropriate use of a college-provided car should be a part of the employment agreement. In an initial contract, moving expenses need to be fully addressed to prevent any surprises for the new president or for the board. Furthermore, opportunities for professional development can be customized to meet the growth needs and career stage of the CEO.

7 *Enhanced Benefits*

The board interested in attracting and retaining a high-performing CEO may want to consider enhanced benefits. These are benefits that are tailored to a president's specific professional and personal needs. Enhanced benefits, which can sometimes become controversial, either through the media or on campus, should be clearly spelled out in the contract. For example, housing allowances, entertainment expenses, charitable contributions, club memberships and dues, and technology and home office needs should be drawn up in such a way that they are defensible in a public forum and meet the cultural norms of the service area. Special benefits that relate to a CEO's particular situation also need to be delineated. Some of these could include child care, financial planning, and domestic partner benefits.

HOUSING OR HOUSING ALLOWANCE

Only a small percentage of community college presidents receive either college-paid housing or a housing allowance as part of their employment contract. In 1998, Vaughan and Weisman wrote, "Nine percent of the current community college presidents live in a college-owned house, a slight decline from 1991 when 10 percent of presidents lived in a college-owned house" (p. 65). The 2002 CCCS showed that only 6% of 383 presidents reported that their contract included provisions for living in a college-owned house; however, another 6% reported living in college-owned housing with the arrangements not part of the contract (AACC, 2002).

The 2006 CCCS shows a marked increase in housing assistance. This may be one important way in which a board can recognize the challenges of moving, particularly to an area with higher housing prices. Of the 483 CEOs who responded to this question, 34% indicated receiving housing or a housing allowance. Of those receiving housing or housing allowance, 123 (75%) had the housing allowance formalized as part of the written contract; 25% received some type of housing benefit, but it was not a part of the contract. Comments from CCCS respondents included "as a condition of employment, the president is required to live on campus," "need to promote housing allowances," and "housing allowance should definitely be included in contract negotiation."

Housing assistance is an issue that is increasingly being discussed by community college boards and CEOs. If the board expects considerable entertaining, fundraising, or other college business to be conducted at the president's home, it is not unreasonable to request a housing allowance. Many presidents prefer a housing allowance over a college-owned home because of the tax advantages of home ownership and the opportunity to build equity, as well as the opportunity to choose a residence that fits their family and lifestyle. There are significant tax benefits and liabilities respecting college-provided housing that can be addressed only by competent legal counsel.

ENTERTAINMENT EXPENSES

Determining the appropriateness of entertainment expenses is a difficult area for many public community college CEOs. They are often expected to entertain visitors and dignitaries in public places and in their homes. Yet many state and local regulations forbid the use of public moneys for food, drinks, and similar expenses. Therefore, presidents find themselves expending considerable personal funds for entertainment expenses that benefit the college. Wherever it is permissible by law, provisions should be made to provide an entertainment allowance or reimbursement for documented entertainment expenses. If public moneys cannot be expended for entertainment, the foundation may step up to provide an entertainment expense allowance for the president.

In some colleges, funds are raised through nonpublic sources, such as vending machine and similar sales. These nonpublic funds can sometimes be used to provide for legitimate entertainment expenses that cannot be covered with public moneys. However, given the complexity of the laws governing the use of such funds, competent counsel should always be consulted before such arrangements are entered into. Because entertainment expenses are most frequently scrutinized and criticized in the media and on campus, it is important to have both the source of such funds and the types of expenses allowed clearly stated as part of a contractual agreement.

As reported in the CCCS, of the 505 respondents to the question about an entertainment expense allowance, 44% did not receive any type of allowance. Of the 56% who did receive an entertainment allowance, only 43% had the terms and conditions of the entertainment allowance spelled out in the contract; 57% indicated that they received an entertainment allowance but that it was not a part of their contract. CEOs and boards who do not clarify the appropriate use of an entertainment allowance may unnecessarily expose themselves to criticism that could be avoided by clear contract language.

CHARITABLE CONTRIBUTIONS

Although presidents should be free to support the charities of their choice, the question becomes—if in a particular context it is desirable as a community leader to make a public contribution to a charity—what funds are to be used? In the CCCS, only 11% of 466 respondents received an allowance for charitable contributions. Of those, 37% had the allowance specifically stated in the contract, and 63% indicated that they received the benefit but it was not a part of the employment contract.

CLUB MEMBERSHIPS

Because of the high-profile position of the CEO in the community, many boards want their CEO to be a member of various social, service, country, city, or athletic clubs. Some such memberships may be requested by the president. Others may be seen as desirable by the board to integrate the president into the community power structure. For example, most CEOs are members of their local Rotary Clubs, and those dues are most often paid by the institution. As reported in the CCCS, 55% of the 486 respondents to the question on service club dues indicated that the college paid for the dues, most often for the Rotary Club. Of those reporting that service club dues were paid, only 38% had paid service club dues as part of the contract; 62% received the benefit, but it was not specifically stated in the contract.

When it comes to country and other social clubs, however, boards may be more aware of and sensitive to public perceptions. Nevertheless, it is important for a community college president to socialize with local business leaders, and, in some communities, clubs are often where such socializing occurs. Thus, if a board wishes its CEO to maintain a leadership role in the community, it may wish to subsidize membership in at least one club where the president can mix and mingle with the movers and shakers in the community, the same people whose goodwill and support can be helpful in moving the college forward. If, as is often the case, state laws or district rules do not permit paying club dues from public moneys, the board may allow foundation or other private sources to be used to support the activity.

Responses to the CCCS indicated that of the 474 respondents to the question on social, recreational, and country club dues, only 28% received these benefits. Of those receiving the benefit, the benefit was stated in the contract for 48%, whereas 52% did not have the benefit stated in the contract. Significantly, 72% of the presidents responding to the CCCS do not receive assistance for social, recreational, or country club dues.

TECHNOLOGY AND HOME OFFICE

Today's community college president is on call 24 hours a day, 7 days a week and is expected to be available when needed. Whether that is good for the president may be debatable, but, like it or not, the technology that increases productivity also means that a president is rarely out of contact. Thus, supplying the major technological devices that make up contemporary communications need to be a part of an employment package. A cell phone and pager, a PDA, a home or laptop computer with appropriate and current software, and high-speed Internet connectivity all should be considered as necessary for the well-connected, technology-savvy president.

Cell phones and laptops have become so ubiquitous that it is hard to imagine a CEO without these tools. Nevertheless, when asked whether they received a cell phone, pager, or both as a benefit of their employment, 16% of respondents indicated that they did not. However, 25% said that they did have a phone as a contract-stated benefit, and 59% indicated that they had a phone but that it was not a part of the contract. Inasmuch as cell phone records are easily captured and can be accessed just as e-mails can in various forms of litigation, it is the wise board that defines the appropriate use of the phone and other college-owned equipment and sets boundaries on personal or outside business use. Of 488 respondents to the question about home office equipment, only 35% indicated that they received home office equipment, services, or both. Of those who did have home office equipment, 35% had such equipment specified in the contract, and 65% indicated that they had such equipment but it was not a part of the contract. Any college-owned property used by the CEO at home or while traveling should be properly accounted for at all times in accordance with state or college policies.

CHILD CARE

As the number of female presidents increases, as well as the number of president's spouses who hold full-time employment outside the home, child care is a benefit a board may want to consider offering. The employment agreement should stipulate the conditions of the child care benefit, dollar limits if appropriate, and whether the benefit includes after-school child care as well as preschool child care. If the president is expected to use child-care facilities at the college, that too should be spelled out.

A noncustodial parent may have periodic child-care needs when he or she has children visiting. There may be needs for travel support to visit minor children. Other special considerations are as varied as the people who occupy the position. The board's sensitivity to such personal and family needs will be appreciated and recognized by a CEO and will engender loyalty to the board and to the institution.

FINANCIAL PLANNING

The board may wish to provide reimbursement for the use of outside financial planners or consultants. CEOs may not have a good understanding of the most advantageous investments of their current and future income and may not have the time or interest to develop the necessary expertise. If the use of an outside financial planner, consultant, or counselor is important to the CEO and the board is in agreement, these benefits should be clearly delineated in the contract, including the details of maximum dollars to be spent, qualifications of service providers, clarifications of possible conflict of interest, and length and conditions of employment.

When current CEOs were asked whether they had access to financial planning as part of their employment agreements, of the 457 responding, a large majority (91%) did not have such a benefit. Only 8% indicated they had such a benefit, and only 1% had the benefit written into their contracts. A provision for an outside financial planner could be an attractive enhanced benefit for a new CEO; it might also be an additional benefit to help retain an effective CEO.

DOMESTIC PARTNERS

In the CCCS, participants were asked whether the college or governing agency offered benefits to domestic partners. Of the 540 responding to the query, 12% indicated that they did not know, 63% indicated that benefits were not available to a domestic partner, and 25% indicated that benefits were available to a domestic partner. In response to what types of benefits were available for domestic partners, there were some limitations reflected in respondents' comments:

- must be registered as domestic partners

- if the domestic partner is same sex per Oregon law

- In Ohio it is not allowed by law.

- If you're asking do they offer benefits to unmarried domestic partners—yes, if opposite sex.

Other responses indicated a more liberal view:

- same benefits as spouse

- health benefits offered to domestic partners

- benefits are available to gay and lesbian partners

- medical coverage

- language used is spouse or domestic partner

- broad language in health benefits allow this option

SUMMARY

Although certain standard benefits are generic to most contracts, it is the enhanced benefits that may customize the contract to meet the needs of an individual person and board. These enhanced benefits are also the types of benefits that cannot be taken for granted outside the context of a contract. Many presidents have received bad press and created problems for the board and the college over the expenses attendant to maintaining a residence. Similarly, entertainment, charitable contributions, and club memberships are often scrutinized and criticized by both the internal college community and the media. Benefits customized specifically to the needs of a particular CEO—such as child care, financial planning, or benefits for domestic partners—need to be addressed as part of the employment agreement. These types of enhanced benefits, if important to a board and president, must be clearly spelled out and willingly defended by the board if controversy arises. Such enhanced benefits are important to a new president, but they may be even more important to a well-established president whose services the board wants to ensure will continue over an extended tenure.

8 The Termination Clause

ALL EMPLOYMENT AGREEMENTS END. THE expiration or termination of a CEO's contract, regardless of cause, is a momentous occasion for the college and for the president. It represents the end of an era and the sure knowledge of change ahead for the institution. If the parting is amicable—for example, is due to retirement or moving to another position after a positive term of office—the end of the president's term is likely to be the occasion for parties, celebrations, and reflections on accomplishments. If the parting is acrimonious—the result of misconduct, board conflicts, or votes of no confidence from the faculty—the resulting upheaval, divisiveness, lawsuits, or bad press can cause long-lasting damage to the reputation of the college. Obviously, it is in the best interest of both the college and the CEO to be sure that the process of termination is not overlooked in an employment agreement.

Boards and presidents are sometimes like people contemplating marriage: They cannot assume anything but a harmonious relationship for the rest of their lives. It seems quite improper, at such a time of joy and anticipation, to discuss what might happen if the parties find they cannot work and live together. Yet this is precisely the time such a discussion is absolutely necessary. As Nason stated,

> The board needs to know that the new president will not desert the ship at short notice, and the president needs assurance that he or she will be given reasonable leave with salary if the axe should fall. The sensible board will anticipate the possibility of trouble, however remote it may seem, and set forth the terms, conditions and circumstances of separation at the time of appointment. (1980, p. 76)

Although the conditions of employment are usually extensive and the term of the appointment is rendered in some detail, exit strategies are not so common. "Term appointments must be tied to some kind of escape system that provides a dignified exit without undue economic penalties. A president should not be expected to expend him- or herself for the good of the cause while everyone else is protected by job security, tenure, or due process considerations"(Kauffman, 1980, p. 97).

To avoid the possibility of undue disruption, costly lawsuits, and potentially negative press, it is critically important that the grounds for termination be stated in the employment agreement: "Probably most important is laying the groundwork for a harmonious parting of the ways. To avoid acrimony, lawsuits, and bad publicity, a president's contract must spell out the circumstances for retirement or other termination and the specifics of separation compensation" (Bornstein, 1998, p. 4). Howard Ende, a former general counsel for Princeton University, would agree. He maintained that the real "value of a well-written presidential contract is most apparent when a board dismisses a president" (cited in Fain, 2006, p. 14b). A well-written termination clause serves the purpose of protecting the CEO, the board, and the college.

It appears that community college CEOs and boards are getting the message about the importance of a termination clause in the contract (AACC, 2002). Several high-visibility board–CEO disputes may have made all parties more aware of the importance of a clearly defined exit strategy. When the first CCCS was conducted in 2002, 43% of CEOs reported that they did not have a termination clause in the contract. By late 2006, when the current CCCS was conducted, only 19% of the CEOs reported that they did not have a termination clause in the contract. One president commented, "I believe that the language of the separation clause is the critical piece in the CEO contract and that it is best to negotiate this in the initial contract." Although the substance of a termination clause will differ according to state and federal laws and local traditions, it is important that the nature of notice, professional improvement plans, severance pay, and the extension of benefits be spelled out.

REASONS FOR TERMINATION

Most employment agreements will address termination under five circumstances: death, disability, resignation, without cause, and for cause. Depending on the jurisdiction, there may be other circumstances or alternative language that describes circumstances necessitating termination. As in all aspects of the employment agreement, it is essential that the section on termination be prepared by competent and experienced legal counsel.

Death

While it is certainly not something a president and board want to dwell on, presidents do die in office. When that happens, the trauma is difficult enough for the college community and the president's family without having uncertainties as to the disposition of salary and benefits, particularly deferred compensation, bonuses, or contractual agreements for family health insurance after retirement. If a CEO dies during his or her term, the employment agreement should specify what benefits accrue to the CEO's survivors and estate. In the CCCS, of those 444 presidents who indicated they had a termination clause in the contract only 21% said that the contract did not have a specific clause for termination due to death.

Disability

In the event that a CEO becomes ill and is unable to perform the duties required of the position, termination due to disability may be the outcome. Clear processes for determining disability and the consequences of a president being declared disabled should be stated in the employment agreement. For example, how long may the president be absent because of illness before his or her employment agreement terminates on the basis of inability to perform the requirements of the office? A well-drafted termination for disability provision will serve as a road map when such an unfortunate event occurs. Of the 444 presidents who indicated that they had a termination clause in the contract, 23% said the contract had a specific clause for termination due to disability.

Mutual Agreement (Resignation)

When a contract is terminated before the ending date because of a president's resignation, there is an expectation that a minimum notice be given. This notice requirement may be as long as a year and as little as 90 days. Resignation before the end of the stated term usually occurs when a CEO has an opportunity to move to another position or has a physical condition that makes continuing in office difficult. In such circumstances, there is the rightful expectation on the part of the board that the president give adequate notice to provide for a smooth transition while a new president is sought. In such a situation, the CEO would ordinarily be paid a salary and benefits only through the date of termination. In the CCCS, 190 respondents (43%) indicated that their contract did contain provisions for mutually agreeing to terminate the contract.

Without Cause

When a CEO is terminated without cause, it is often because of a change in the board's direction, a change in the external environment, the perceived need for new leadership, or a more serious problem with the performance of the president that nonetheless is deemed better handled through a no-fault termination. Indeed, it should be noted that a termination without cause does not necessarily mean that the president has substantially fulfilled contractual responsibilities or has not engaged in inappropriate activities to the detriment of the college or its reputation. Nor, however, does it imply the opposite. Depending on the terms of the employment agreement, a termination without cause may result in the college's buying out all or a portion of the remaining term of the contract, or, if the president is employed on at at-will basis, his or her compensation may end with a far shorter (or no) payment beyond the termination date. The terms of the employment agreement, as well as federal (and, in some jurisdictions, state) law guide the board's obligations regarding health and other benefits. Of the 444 respondents who indicated they had a termination clause as part of the contract, 26% had a clause for termination without cause.

For Cause

When a CEO is dismissed for cause before the ending date of a contract, it usually implies a serious breach of conduct. At least from the viewpoint of the board, the president has failed to carry out the responsibilities and duties that are delineated by the contract, by board policy, or by state policy. Furthermore, if the president acts in a way that brings discredit to the institution or engages in acts that are morally or fiscally reprehensible, a board may choose to terminate the president for cause. This action should be taken only as a last resort when absolutely necessary to preserve the reputation of the college. The contract terms defining the bases for a termination for cause must be drafted carefully and with the assistance of competent counsel. Likewise, the procedures for initiating a for-cause termination must be described fully in the employment agreement (or, if applicable, in the state law or district policy). As might be expected, for cause is the termination issue that generates the greatest concern among boards and CEOs. This concern was reflected in the CCCS, with 72% of the respondents indicating the inclusion of a provision in the contract dealing with termination for cause.

TERMINATION ISSUES

A number of significant issues are associated with the termination of a contract. Three of the most common are the provision of severance pay, the ability to buy out a contract, and the availability of outplacement services. In the CCCS, of the 444 respondents who had termination clauses as part of the employment agreement, 13% indicated provisions under which severance pay would be provided,

16% indicated provisions under which a contract could be bought out, and only 1 respondent indicated the availability of any kind of outplacement services.

SUMMARY

The acrimonious termination of a contract can be an extremely painful and public affair resulting in damage to the reputation of the CEO, the board, and the college. Rather than all parties simply hoping for the best, the initial employment agreement should specify the terms and conditions under which a contract may be terminated. A contract can be terminated for a variety of legitimate reasons. Sometimes it is at the request of the president; sometimes it is at the request of the board. Most contracts will delineate at least five circumstances under which the contract may be terminated: death, disability, resignation, without cause, and for cause. The conditions and consequences of each type of termination should be specified in the contract. Because of the many legal ramifications as well as the complexity of the termination clause, qualified and experienced legal counsel should be involved to protect the interests of both the board and the CEO.

9 Mediation and Arbitration

IN THIS CHAPTER, INFORMATION IS given that will help CEOs seek wider latitude in introducing features in their employment agreement during contract negotiations with boards of trustees. Such latitude usually narrows in subsequent years. In most cases, possible points of dispute or conflict, even instances that could lead to termination, are not discussable during contract negotiation. Employers can incur high costs when long-duration disputes must be resolved. The costs to CEOs, however, are even greater in proportion to net assets. A CEO's financial well-being can be damaged, as well as his or her self-esteem and professional reputation, in the event of a long court resolution. The following fictional case study is offered to illustrate the effects of resolving disputes through litigation.

ACCEPTING THE JOB

Murray Smith had worked as a professional administrator in three well-known and reputable community college districts. Each promotion followed a period of long dedication and achievement as a dean, a provost, and a vice chancellor for academic affairs. Smith's elevation to a chancellor's position in a large multicollege district was a natural capstone to an already impressive career as a professional administrator. After doing some investigating and receiving a search consulting

The material in this chapter was contributed by Paul A. Elsner. Elsner served for 23 years as chancellor of the 10-college Maricopa County Community College District. Since retiring in 1999, he has served in various consulting and advisory capacities to boards of governors, regents, and executive leaders. His academic background includes a doctorate from Stanford University and the completion of study at Harvard's Institute for Educational Advancement.

firm's invitation to apply for a position with a large urban community college district, Smith agreed to interviews with the faculty-based screening committee, community advisors, and the district's governing board.

The extensive screening and interview process resulted in a $325,000 offer to preside over a seven-campus system as chancellor. Smith had basically decided to take the position, but he asked for a week's delay on the decision to discuss matters with his wife, former mentors, and colleagues. He assured the district that he would respond in 7 days or less.

The advice he received from his mentors was not particularly in depth. One former supervisor urged demanding the highest salary going into the job, stating that as years of service go by, leverage lessens—especially with resources generally more and more difficult to secure. Another said to insist on a 4-year rolling contract and to negotiate salary and other conditions after each year of service. This meant to Smith that at any given year he would either have a 4-year contract in hand or the ability to achieve a minimum of 3 years of salary. Failure to achieve a rollover was a signal to start looking for a different job.

Smith accepted the job, and for 3 years he enjoyed successful rollovers, ensuring 4 more years of compensated employment after each year. Moreover, cost-of-living allowances and even an adjustment on the base salary placed his salary at $465,000 in his fourth year. This did not include increased car, housing, and health benefits and annuity and retirement compensations. In all, the salary plus benefits exceeded $635,000 in the last year of the newly negotiated 4-year contract. Things looked good for Smith.

UNFORESEEN DEVELOPMENTS

In the last months of the first year of his last 4-year contract, Smith received a complaint from an employee through the district's compliance division that certain equipment inventories and payments to vendors and one consultant had not been adequately documented at the federal compliance review. Moreover, the grant from the U.S. Office of Education had been applied for and received 7 years back, even before Smith had come aboard. In addition, Smith approached the reporting employee with obvious anger and an irritable demeanor, even suggesting negligence on her part and on the part of those of her co-workers who were involved.

Five weeks after he had stormed into, and, a half-hour later, out of the reporting employee's office, the human resource office and the state and federal compliance review agencies filed a complaint against Smith for retaliating against a whistle-blowing employee and sexually harassing the same employee. After several weeks of haranguing and stalemate, about which the board was at first only loosely informed, the board met in executive session with the district's special counsel and notified Smith of dismissal for cause. Three counts were specified:

1. Failure to fully inform the board in either a timely or a thorough manner concerning federal compliance shortcomings.

2. Mismanagement of detail and information gathering after learning of federal grant noncompliance. Resorting to anger and belittling an earnest employee reporting information about which the chancellor should be receptive.

3. Retaliation against and sexual harassment of a whistle-blowing employee.

Smith, in shock, received this notice by certified mail on the Saturday of a weekend he had hoped to enjoy. That Monday morning, Smith took personal leave to visit his family lawyer. He was referred to a practicing attorney in civil dispute resolution.

On the following Monday, he met with the board and presented his analysis of the situation, stressing that the federal grant was received at least 2 years before he took office. He also emphasized that he may have approached the matter with anger and did not take into account the fact that the office workers may have experienced stress. He said that he returned to the clerical unit to apologize to at least three of the employees in the compliance office.

Finally, he accounted for the loss of compensation if the board dismissed him. He submitted an analysis to the board that showed at least $1.5 million in lost compensation for the duration of the rollover contract if 3.5 years of compensation were taken from him. He also stated that on the advice of his attorney he would petition the courts for such compensation as a result of wrongful dismissal. The board's reaction was silence.

At the following regular board meeting, the board—as a committee of the whole board from executive session—passed a resolution in support of Smith's dismissal, by a vote of seven in favor to one opposed, with one abstaining among the nine-member board. The board did allocate $125,000 to Smith for relocation benefits and allowed 3 months of temporary office space, a phone, and a fax for his personal use. With his attorney, Smith filed a petition for $1.5 million in recovery of lost compensation and court costs in superior court. He felt that he should waive punitive damages and recover lost earnings only.

The trial lasted 9 weeks and was held over for technical reasons of argument for another 6 weeks before a judge ruled in favor of the board's decision and ordered that legal and court costs be borne by both parties, which in Smith's case exceeded $350,000, including the cost of depositions and expert witnesses.

REEXAMINING THE CASE

On examining the resources of the employing district and its board, Smith learned that the board was well prepared for judicial proceedings in several ways:

- The district had a contract agreement with a prestigious law firm with locations in the two major cities of the state and an open account to deploy either office. The firm had extensive experience handling nuisance litigation, personnel and labor negotiations, and protracted cases that stalled or remained unresolved.

- Another law firm consulted by the district specialized in property and capital disputes and litigation.

- The district had liability insurance that covered the cost of litigation when cases exceeded $300,000 in documented legal costs. It also had personal liability insurance for all principals in executive classifications and for board members. (As a litigant, Smith forfeited that liability protection.)

It was obvious that Smith and his attorney failed to see that a huge urban college district had deep pocket capacity to withstand long litigation and court battle, compared with Smith, whose major resources were his small savings, equity in his home, and his retirement pension, which he unfortunately was forced to invade. This case study—although fiction—does reflect some measure of reality. These realities include the following:

- Most college CEOs cannot afford long, protracted litigation.

- Organizations, whether corporate, private, public, or government—such as a municipality or even a school district—can and often do have huge resources to withstand and secure petitions for relief in the courts.

- Wrongful dismissal occurs too often, but wrongful is hard to prove.

REWRITING THE CASE

So, how might Smith's case be different if it could be rewritten? Begin with the following assumptions:

- Smith took too little time to assess his chances against a monolithic and well-arsenaled district, at least in terms of the legal forces that could be deployed.

- Smith held to the board's obligations of his contract, but they included basically only the financial obligation of the employing party.

- Provisions for cause or justification for cause, in this case dismissal, were not referred to in Smith's contract. Either the attorney had none to invoke or none were present in the contract.

Can we assume that Smith went for the compensation as he was advised by his mentors? His contract paid well, but was he protected? We do not know the answers here, of course. If we assume it was merely a compensation and duration contract, indeed Smith had considerable exposure to what happened. If we assume that he had the usual conditions on which dismissal is based—moral turpitude and conviction of a felony, usually the two extreme conditions for dismissal—would he have had a better case?

Probably not, unfortunately. But if moral turpitude were an expressed condition in the contract, certainly sexual harassment had allegedly occurred. But such cases fade after the depositions start flying back and forth, and usually complainants carry the burden of proof. The defendants can plead denial down to insensitivity and admit to a need for consciousness raising as a therapeutic measure. Moreover, Smith's outburst occurred in the compliance office, and he was there only for a few minutes.

As to a felony, none is evident, but malfeasance may have occurred on his watch—he had served only 1½ of the years of the duration of the grant. Whose malfeasance? The previous administration's? But one reality remains: If the board strikes as it did to dismiss, the burden falls on Smith to disprove cause.

AVOIDING COURT RESOLUTION

There may be many reasons or circumstances that justify resolution of conflict in court. But generally, the odds stack up much like those in Smith's fictional case. To avoid court resolution, what are the options? Generally, they fall in three categories: (1) mediation, (2) arbitration, and (3) combinations of mediation and arbitration. But it is important that all three start with the basic employment contract between the hiring authority and the employee. It is important that the hiring authority specify the municipality, college, school district, state, or board of university regents—whichever is the only hiring (and firing) authority that exists.

If an arbitration clause or mediation provision is included in the contract, it is wise to specify that it is an employee's right to invoke the clause, requiring the board to comply with granting a mediation or arbitration process to the employee. There is justification for the chancellor, president, or superintendent of a school or college district to be the only one granted mediation rights. Usually such professional positions operate under a single contract. Therefore, a "right to demand arbitration" clause should appear in the contract of employment. One also should state clearly that if mediation is the employee's choice, that arbitration can be resorted to in the case of mediative impasse. Some states may prohibit binding arbitration, but generally both the employee and the board have to assess whether they want to bind each other on the arbitration outcome.

Had Smith had a provision for requiring mediation or arbitration, he may not have needed to exhaust his personal resources in litigation. Although no guarantee of avoiding deep costs, arbitration might increase the probability of reaching a settlement sooner. In addition, the degree of settlement could have been more in Smith's favor. If there were a binding arbitration clause, he might have prevailed on all amounts due him over the duration of his contract—a considerable sum.

Let us speculate that the board's dismissal action was highly questionable. For fictional case study purposes, assume that the following occurred:

- The named compliance office employee who filed the sexual harassment charge had a history of lodging and exploiting sexual harassment charges against employers. None were taken up by the Equal Employment Opportunity Commission officer of either the district or the state. All involved legal review by experienced counsel.

- Smith did not recall ever encountering the complainant, except in his explosion of anger in the compliance department, an office of three full-time and one part-time employee. Smith readily admitted to showing anger. He expressed regret to the board, the compliance department, and the general accounting office.

- On Smith's arrival as chancellor, he had visited the whole accounting division, which included the three full-time and one part-time compliance specialists, and said that in his preliminary review of budgeting and accounting practices, he had indicated that he was troubled by the "posting lag" of both accounts receivable and accounts payable. He added that he attributed this matter to staff sitting on paper processing and that he directed all staff to move their transactions and accounting activity so that they would not incur postings after a fiscal year closeout. Such past fiscal year postings do occur, so Smith directed that late postings must be routinely brought before the governing board. This policy was successfully implemented.

We could assume then that Smith's anger resulted from his frustration with the fact that proper procedures were not put into place under his watch. Showing anger was inappropriate; following up on tighter procedures after examining a problem was appropriate. Smith felt he had done the latter thoroughly and professionally.

No provisions for mediation or arbitration existed in Smith's contract. His resolution had been litigation and a court's review and decision. He felt that accepting a $125,000 relocation settlement was unfair to him. It is obvious that he was too underresourced and disadvantaged in legal capacity to compete with a huge district and its experienced legal experts.

Mediation and arbitration both involve the development of third (neutral) parties, but the procedures are not the same. In the Smith case, the board acted unilaterally. The mediative process could hardly apply. Mediation implies a good-faith attempt to resolve a dispute by requiring both parties to come to the table. But arbitration especially binds; arbitration usually can and probably should follow an attempt to resolve matters of dispute. Resolution is in the hands of the arbitrator. The arbitrator reviews arguments and circumstances and determines the procedures of the process; he or she reviews, studies, and decides. Arbitration can be expensive, but it is regarded as a faster, more private and confidential process.

The advantage for Smith and the board of trustees is the opportunity to reach a settlement without weeks, even months, of adverse publicity. For Smith, this could mean less risk of having his professional reputation devalued in the CEO search marketplace. For the board, either appointed or elected, adverse publicity issues have political costs.

SUMMARY

In the interest of time and personal resources, both public and private arbitration processes stand as more sensible alternatives to the costly and often painful ordeal of a long-duration court trial. Arbitration clauses are exceptionally complex, often covering several pages of an employment agreement. They must be drafted by competent counsel, and each side—the president and the board—must have its own attorneys approve of the language. Only a well-qualified attorney can offer the specific advice, language, and provisions appropriate to a particular situation, institution, and participants.

10 *Ethics and Leadership*

CEOS AND BOARDS HAVE A responsibility to the communities they serve to provide exemplary ethical leadership. "At any level, in any sector in society, a public leader automatically takes on the responsibility of moral or ethical leadership" (Vaughan, 1992, p. 53). Those at the top set the tone for the entire institution. The relationship between the board chair and the president is particularly crucial. Trust, high expectations, and personal integrity are paramount. The development of a meaningful CEO contract provides an opportunity for the board and the CEO to demonstrate their commitment to engage in ethical behavior for the benefit of all of the community.

In the *AGB Statement on Board Accountability*, AGB (2007) has emphasized the ethical responsibilities of boards, pointing out that "lapses and failures in the integrity and governance of certain participants in the nonprofit and higher education communities—particularly in such areas as conflict of interest, executive compensation, and financial oversight—have raised troubling questions" (p. 1). AGB maintains that governing boards of public institutions, whether their members are elected or appointed, ultimately derive their authority from the people of the state and are thus accountable to the people of the state. Boards have a responsibility to regularly assess not only the CEO's performance but also the performance of the board as a whole and of trustees. Communities, both internal and external, are watching the way top leaders—boards and CEOs—deal with financial issues, the business community, the purchasing of equipment and supplies, the hiring and

---

Some material from this chapter also appears in a chapter by Desna Wallin in *Ethical Leadership in the Community College: Bridging Theory and Daily Practice* (Wallin, 2007).

firing of personnel, student standards, the academic quality of the institution, and the overall morale of the faculty and staff.

CODES OF ETHICS

Ethical leadership is essential to keeping the trust of both internal and external constituencies, including funding agencies and legislative bodies. AGB urges every board to "adopt a statement that addresses the values, principles, and expectations of members. Each member of the board should affirm his or her understanding of and commitment to board and trustee responsibilities" (2007, p. 6).

Through its Presidents Academy, AACC has recognized the impact of presidential leadership and proposed a "Recommended Code of Ethics for Chief Executive Officers of Community Colleges." The code begins with a preamble that states, in part,

> *The Chief Executive Officer ... helps to determine ethical standards for his/ her institution through personal conduct and institutional leadership ... is expected to maintain the highest ethical standards through individual actions and decisions within the institution and to expect adherence to the same standards by Boards of Trustees, administrators, faculty, staff and students. (AACC, 2005)*

The document goes on to suggest that a set of core values can help foster ethical standards that permeate the institution. The values begin with four basic standards. Others, specific to the institution and its history and needs, may be added as appropriate. The CEO should strive to promote these four values as a starting point in all colleges:

- trust and respect for all individuals

- honesty in all actions

- just and fair treatment of all people

- integrity in all actions (AACC, 2005)

The code also addresses a CEO's specific responsibilities to various constituencies, including board members, administrators, faculty and staff, students, other educational institutions, business and civic groups, and the community at large. The code concludes with a description of the rights and expectations of CEOs, including a right to having clear expectations of performance from the board; the right to select the management team; the right to participate in setting goals and policies; and the right to a clear written contract that outlines the conditions of employment, method of evaluation, and level of compensation (AACC, 2005). In its "Standards of Good Practice for Trustee Boards," ACCT (2007) also addresses ethics, emphasizing "that [a board's] behavior, and that of its members, exemplify ethical behavior and conduct that is above reproach" and "that [a board] endeavors to remain always accountable to the community."

ETHICAL ISSUES

Countless ethical issues confront CEOs and boards every working day. Davis (2003) delineated a plethora of potential ethical issues that should be of concern to any president. Within the institution there are decisions made about student admissions, particularly in high-demand programs, in relation to equity and access. There are issues concerning the availability of a variety of forms of financial aid and the relationship of the institution to the agencies that provide financial aid. Colleges have not always held strictly to truth in marketing the college, enrollment figures, placement of students, and other services and programs. The appointment, promotion, and reward of faculty, as well as student–faculty relationships, exemplify ethical issues. Academic honesty, student grading and testing, classroom teaching, and the preparation of letters of recommendation for students suggest additional ethical issues. Student-related issues include tolerance of diversity in student behavior, appearance, and values; academic honor codes; and disciplinary processes.

Institutional policies, created by boards and implemented by the CEO, present another opportunity to examine the ethics of the institution. Are there well-established processes for the reporting of sexual harassment and criminal activities? Are there unambiguous due-process procedures in place? Are there clear expectations about the use of college property, including telephone, copy machines, and laptops for personal use? Internet use? College travel and reimbursement policies?

Outside the institution there are ethical issues related to community linkages and to business and industry alliances and partnerships. There are political issues in relation to local, regional, and state policymakers; donations and appearances at fundraisers; and political activities on behalf of candidates. Ethical issues are frequently raised in relation to governing boards. "No aspect of a governing board's activity is more visible than the conduct of its business as a board. If serious lapses occur at the highest level of the institution's governance, confidence in overall institutional management inevitably will suffer" (AGB, 2007, p. 4).

Boards must ask themselves difficult but important questions. Do board members benefit financially through business interests relative to their position with the college? Are all possible conflicts of interest recognized and dealt with openly? Are there opportunities for undue influence concerning hiring and firing of employees? Because of the high visibility and the importance of the example that they set, board members "must be individually accountable to one another for civility, preparedness, ethical behavior, restraint, cohesion, and sound judgment" (AGB, 2007, p. 4).

The increasing need to raise funds to enhance the operations of the college, to support faculty, and to provide financial aid to students can also be a source of ethical dilemmas. How active should the president be in raising funds? What is the role of the board, both as an entity and as individual members? What can be promised to donors? What should and should not be promised? How should funds be invested for the good of the college? Who should be selected as the college banking entity? Who is responsible for investment decisions? How do the president and the board know that all such decisions are being made ethically, with the best interests of the college foremost?

PRINCIPLES OF ETHICAL LEADERSHIP

Northouse (2007) set out five basic principles of ethical leadership that are directly applicable to the role of the contemporary community college CEO and board:

1. respecting others

2. serving others

3. being just

4. being honest

5. building community

Ethical presidents and boards respect others as ends, not as means to an end. They are empathetic and tolerant and give credence to the views and interests of others within and without the institution. The president, in particular, is a good listener who is willing, when appropriate, to defer to others.

Ethical presidents and boards serve others and put others' needs above personal needs or personal gain. Employees are empowered to perform their work with a minimum of oversight. Mentoring is apparent as experienced employees help new employees become a part of the culture of the institution. Teams and team building are valued. "Ethical leaders have a responsibility to attend to others, be of service to them, and make decisions pertaining to them that are beneficial and not harmful to their welfare" (Northouse, 2007, p. 352).

Ethical presidents and boards are just. Issues of fairness and justice are a top priority in dealing with one another and in dealing with faculty and staff. The distribution of resources in an institution reveals whether or not decisions are just. Favoritism has no place. Inasmuch as resources are always finite, and there will always be competition for those resources, a just president must consider principles involved in distributive justice. These principles are applied in different situations and include allotting resources on the basis of equal shares, according to individual need, according to the person's rights, according to individual effort, according to societal contribution, and according to merit (Northouse, 2007).

Ethical presidents and boards are honest. Although this seems obvious, it is not always so easy. When a president or board member is shown to be dishonest, the institution experiences distrust. The president and board may be seen as undependable, unreliable, and not worthy of following. Honesty goes beyond simply telling the truth, even if it is painful. Honesty also implies an openness to discussing what matters to the institution and to employees. It means that decisions are based on evidence, that policies are clear, and that the budgeting process is transparent. An honest president is authentic and is sensitive to the needs and feelings of others and tempers honesty with consideration. An honest president will reward openly honest behavior in the organization and welcome information that may be negative or uncomfortable. An honest president or board member does not shoot the messenger!

Ethical presidents and boards actively build community. They recognize the need to attend to broader community needs, within the institution and within the area served by the college. An ethical president and board recognize that it is not beneficial in the long term to impose ideas and actions on others. Rather, it is specifically the role of the ethical president to move leaders and followers toward a common goal so that both are changed in a positive way.

This type of leadership is referred to as transformational leadership (Burns, 1978). Burns suggested that successful leadership is grounded in the leader–follower relationship. It cannot be controlled solely by the leader and does not involve coercion. According to Northouse, "An ethical leader takes into account the purposes of everyone involved in the group and is attentive to the interests of the community and the culture" (2007, p. 356). The CEO and board who set out to build community must work to ensure that individual and group goals support and sustain the common public good.

SUMMARY

Consciously striving to live an ethical life is challenging in itself. But it is much more challenging to carry the responsibility for the well-being of people as well as an institution when serving in the role of a community college CEO or a board member. It is at once a great privilege and opportunity and a great burden. Those who occupy the community college presidency, as well as those who serve conscientiously as board members, have a special responsibility because of their visibility in the community and their positional power to exercise that power ethically. The development of the CEO contract and its implications provide a highly visible venue for boards and CEOs to convey ethical obligations to stakeholders.

Ethical presidents and ethical boards are not perfect. They make mistakes and they acknowledge those mistakes. They set an example for the institution by showing respect for others, serving others, being just and honest, and actively building community. They have thoughtfully devised their own meaningful codes of ethics and use those codes to underpin all decisions they make. They are open in their dealings with their colleagues and with leaders in the community. They are sensitive to the needs of others and genuinely care about others. Strong, strategic, well-prepared community college presidents and boards are needed to effectively serve the diverse and dynamic institutions that community colleges have become. Particularly in today's challenging political and fiscal environments, as colleges increasingly operate globally, boards and CEOs must be accountable to their constituencies and scrupulously ethical in all their dealings.

11 *A Successful Tenure*

A CAREFUL READING OF THE previous 10 chapters should make apparent the fact that there is no such thing as a one-size-fits-all standard employment agreement. There may be certain standard provisions, but each employment agreement is its own work of art, crafted and tailored to the needs and expectations of the president, the board, and important internal and external constituencies. It is imperative to understand that the most significant factor leading to a successful presidential tenure is not having an employment agreement with fine legal phrasing, not a spectacular salary, not a cornucopia of benefits, not even the detailed expectations of the board. The most critical element necessary for a successful presidential tenure is the confidence and trust between a board and a president. There can be no substitute for integrity, honesty, and open communication.

That being said, however, it is equally important to capture the sense of trust and enthusiasm that exists at the beginning of a presidency and put it into a written agreement. Human nature being what it is, people remember events and conversations differently. They interpret the same promises differently. And they may develop honest differences in their vision of the direction in which the college should move. A written agreement to which all parties concur can save a president, a board, and a college from unnecessary embarrassment, bitterness, and public wrangling. More important, the existence of a written employment agreement that gives a reasonable expectation of continued employment for a period of time frees a president to tackle difficult and sensitive situations and to make hard decisions without the fear that displeasing a powerful person or group may result in unemployment on short notice.

A well-written employment agreement will contain four basic components: the term of the appointment, the compensation package including salary and benefits, the evaluation process, and termination procedures. Even the simplest employment agreements should address these four components in enough detail to ensure complete clarity and understanding. Often the president and the board are most focused on salary and benefits. That, too, is what the public, the college community, and the media are most interested in scrutinizing. Standard benefits such as insurance of various kinds, leave policies, car use, relocation expenses, and professional development activities should be spelled out to avoid any misunderstanding or confusion. When a board deems it appropriate to provide enhanced benefits, such as club memberships, entertainment expenses, and housing allowances, there is the natural tendency to think it best not to reduce to writing what could potentially bring criticism to the board and the college.

The temptation simply to arrive at a verbal understanding should be avoided at all costs. Many presidents can attest to the hasty retreat, the claims of misunderstanding, and the bad case of amnesia that can overcome a board when the public to whom it is accountable begins to criticize certain actions and expenses. The CEO, too, may genuinely misunderstand the latitude given by the board. The board chair, in the role of spokesperson for the board, must exercise strong leadership and be willing to justify any and all perks extended to the president in terms of a competitive market, board expectations, and performance.

The use of a compensation committee in determining salary and benefits is highly recommended. The committee should exercise due diligence in researching and understanding competitive CEO packages in comparable community colleges. The compensation committee should carefully document its processes and ensure that the entire board speaks as one entity and is entirely supportive before offering a compensation package.

The president needs to have a clear understanding of the expectations of the board and the performance measures by which he or she will be judged. CEOs have limited time and unlimited demands on that time; it is crucial that they know where to spend their time to make the greatest impact and meet the expectations of the board. Written standards, expectations, goals, and objectives, as well as evaluation time lines and processes, should be a part of the employment agreement.

A good employment agreement will always include a well-crafted termination clause. Because all employment agreements end, it is foolhardy in the extreme to fail to plan for that ending. The board should specify the conditions under which the agreement will be terminated and the consequences of each. Boards should consider alternative dispute resolution in the form of arbitration and mediation to avoid most costly and time-consuming litigation and the negative publicity that accompanies such public disagreements.

"CEO's jobs are highly risky, and that is simply part of the landscape." That comment by a perceptive president responding to the 2006 CCCS is unarguably true. Those who are risk averse should not even consider a community college presidency. Having a model contract, with clearly delineated expectations, will not eliminate that risk. A strong contract can, however, temper the risk and free a president to devote time and energy to leading the institution and making difficult decisions.

Boards, too, can know that the direction for the college has been clearly set and the expectations of the board have been communicated to the president through a well-written employment agreement. Just as boards are becoming more selective and sophisticated in knowing what they expect of a president, the number of qualified candidates may be declining because of retirements and quality of life issues. In the next decade it will be more important than ever for boards to develop and offer competitive compensation packages if they hope to attract and retain high-performing presidents and CEOs.

Keeping a good CEO is as important to a board as getting the right one in the first place. In fact it has been suggested that

> progress toward educational excellence is hindered by a merry-go-round of presidents. If you change CEOs all the time, you never give your college the chance to develop and stick with a long term plan. If the CEO is moving the college's educational agenda forward, the board should do everything possible to keep that streak going. A board can be effective only if the CEO is effective. (Jensen, Giles, & Kirklin, 2000, pp. 66–67)

One way to keep that successful streak going is for the board to pay close attention to offering a competitive salary and benefits package as part of a well-constructed employment agreement.

The board–CEO relationship is absolutely critical to the success of any community college. Respecting their separate but complementary roles, the partnership between a committed board and a dedicated president can provide tremendous educational opportunities to the people and communities they serve. CEOs and boards need to hold to high ethical standards as expected by their constituencies. Working together, with mutual trust, integrity, and sense of purpose, boards and presidents can bring to their communities education, training, and services to provide a better future and help fulfill the promise of America's community colleges.

$\mathcal{A}$ppendix:
$\mathcal{S}$urvey $\mathcal{I}$nstrument

2006 CEO CONTRACT AND COMPENSATION SURVEY

Note: This survey was distributed in an online format. It has been reformatted here to serve as a resource for this publication.

1. **Please confirm that you are responding from (ID - specific college information) (Required)**

   ☐ Yes ☐ No

   Employment Contract

2. **What type of appointment/job agreement do you have? (Required)**

   ☐ Formal contract ☐ Letter of agreement ☐ Neither

   Additional comments:

   Note: If "neither" is selected. respondent is directed to Question #2a, however, if "formal contract" or "letter of agreement" is selected, respondent proceeds to Question #3.

   2a. **If you do not have a contract is the reason:**

   ☐ Board preference

   ☐ Contracts not allowed by state law

   ☐ Contract not allowed by system

   ☐ Report to chancellor/president, not a board

   ☐ Other

If you selected other, please specify:

2b.   How concerned are you about the lack of a contract? (Select one)
☐ Very Concerned   ☐ Concerned   ☐ Not Concerned

Additional comments:

Note: After completed Question # 2b, the respondent goes directly to the "Compensation & Benefits" section of the survey, beginning with question #11.

Duties and responsibilities:

3.   Which of the following duties and responsibilities are specifically spelled out in your formal contract/ letter of agreement? (check all that apply)
☐ Academic leadership   ☐ Community leadership
☐ Fundraising responsibilities   ☐ Business and industry partnerships
☐ Public school partnerships   ☐ Authority for hiring and firing
☐ Communicating with the board
☐ Perform a role with the board (secretary, treasurer, etc.
☐ Other duties and responsibilities (Please explain)

Term of Contract:

4.   What month does your formal contract/letter of agreement year begin: (Select one)
☐ January   ☐ February   ☐ March   ☐ April   ☐ May   ☐ June
☐ July   ☐ August   ☐ September ☐ October   ☐ November ☐ December

5.   What is the term of your employment? (Select one)
☐ One year   ☐ Two years   ☐ Three years ☐ Four years ☐ Five years
☐ Indefinite ☐ Other
If you selected other, please specify:

6.   Do you have a rolling agreement? If yes, please describe below.
☐ Yes   ☐ No

Additional comments:

Evaluation:

7. **What type of specific board-conducted evaluation requirement is in your formal contract/letter of agreement?**

   ☐ No evaluation requirement   ☐ Annually
   ☐ Near the end of the contract period   ☐ Other

   If you selected other, please specify:

8. **Are there specific criteria spelled out in your contract / letter of agreement that will form the basis for your evaluation?**

   ☐ Yes   ☐ No

   If so, please list those criteria.

Termination:

9. **Which of the following termination clauses are specified in your formal contract / letter of agreement?**

   ☐ For cause   ☐ Without cause
   ☐ Mutual agreement   ☐ Disability
   ☐ Death   ☐ Severance pay
   ☐ Contract buy out   ☐ Outplacement services
   ☐ No termination clause is specified   ☐ Other

   If you selected other, please specify:

Compensation and Benefits:

10. **Is your compensation level specified in your contract/agreement?**

    ☐ Yes   ☐ No

Salary information:

AACC WILL NOT share individual salary figures with any third party. Salary data will be reported in aggregate form with a minimum of five responses.

11. **Please DO NOT use commas in numeric data fields.**

    Current year base salary $
    Previous year base salary $

12. Is there a written process for you to receive raises?

☐ Yes　　☐ No

13. Which of the following criteria are considered (check all that apply)?

☐ Raise is based on meritorious service

☐ Raise is based on achievement of specifically-stated goals

☐ Raise is based on state increases

☐ Raise is based on other employees' increases

☐ Raise is received in regular increments

☐ Raise is given at the discretion of the Board

14. Did you receive a bonus when agreeing to take your current position (i.e. signing bonus)?

☐ Yes　　☐ No

15. Are retention bonuses offered to you? If yes, please explain below.

☐ Yes　　☐ No

Additional comments:

16. Are you eligible for any other bonus or incentive pay?

☐ Yes　　☐ No

Note: If "yes", respondent proceeds to Question #16a. If "no", respondent proceeds to Question #17

16a. What is the amount of the bonuses received in your previous contract year?

Amount provided by the college　　　　　　　　$

Amount provided by the foundation or other sources　　$

16b. Please indicate which performance measures your bonuses may be based on (check all that apply).

☐ Bonuses are not based on performance

☐ Endowment/fundraising

☐ Financial performance (e.g., cost containment)

☐ Enrollment increases

☐ Student success measures

☐ Achievement of other specifically-stated goals

☐ Exemplary or meritorious service (beyond contract)

☐ Board evaluation

☐ peer college review

☐ Other

If you selected other, please specify:

17. If you received any other cash compensation arising from your responsibilities as college president in the past contract year, please indicate the amount received from each source below.

Amount provided by college $

Amount provided by foundation $

Amount from other sources $

18. If you received any cash compensation for activities outside of your regular responsibilities as college president in the past contract year, please indicate the amount earned from each activity below.

Consulting services $

Service on paid boards $

Honoraria for speeches and presentations $

Other outside compensation $

19. What restrictions, if any, are placed on your outside earnings (check all that apply)?

☐ No restrictions

☐ Number of days per year is limited

☐ Amount of money earned is limited

☐ Required to take vacation to perform services

☐ Other

If you selected other, please specify:

20. Please indicate which of the following insurance benefits are offered to you and whether or not they are written into your contract.

Benefit	Offered and Paid 100%	Offered and Paid Partially	Offered but Not Paid	Not Offered	In Contract
Medical					
Prescription drug					
Dental					
Hearing					
Vision					
Employee life insurance					
Short-term disability (STD)					

Long-term care (LTC)

Accidental death
and dismemberment

Travel accident insurance

21. **Please indicate which of the following insurance benefits are offered to your dependents and whether or not they are written into your contract.**

Benefit	Offered and Paid 100%	Offered and Paid Partially	Offered but Not Paid	Not Offered	In Contract
Medical					
Prescription drug					
Dental					
Hearing					
Vision					
Life insurance					

22. **Please indicate which of the following allowances are available to you and whether or not they are written into your contract.**

Benefit	Receive/ In Contract	Receive/ Not In Contract	Do not receive
Car or car allowance			
Housing or housing allowance			
Cell phone/pager			
Financial counseling			
Home office equipment and services			
Service club dues (e.g., Rotary)			
Social/ recreational/ country club dues			
Allowance for entertaining expenses			
Allowance for charitable contributions			
Allowance for political fundraisers			

23. **Which of the following allowances are available to your spouse/domestic partner (check all that apply)?**

☐ Use of the college car   ☐ Entertainment expenses
☐ Travel expenses   ☐ Other

If you selected other, please specify:

24. **Please describe below any other allowances or benefits you or your spouse receive and indicate whether or not they are written into your contract.**

25. **Does your college and/or governing agency offer benefits to domestic partners? Please explain below.**

    ☐ Yes   ☐ No   ☐ Don't know

    Additional comments:

    Leave:

26. **How many days of paid leave do you earn each year for each of the following?**

    Personal leave   _____ days

    Vacation (exclude holidays)   _____ days

    Sick leave   _____ days

    Disability leave (exclude FMLA)   _____ days

27. **As president, are you eligible for sabbatical leave?**

    ☐ Yes   ☐ No

28. **Please indicate the terms and requirements of your sabbatical (e.g., one semester at full pay, one year at half pay, sabbatical may be taken after seven years of full-time employment).**

29. **What incentives are provided to participate in professional development? Are these incentives written into your contract/agreement?**

    Retirement:

30. **Which of the following retirement benefits are offered to you (check all that apply)?**

    ☐ Defined contribution plan (e.g., 403(b) or 401(k))

    ☐ Defined benefit plan (i.e., pension)

    ☐ Supplemental executive retirement plan

    ☐ Continued health insurance plan

    ☐ Deferred compensation plan

    ☐ Other

If you selected other, please specify:

31. What percent of your annual base salary is contributed to your retirement plan by the college or foundation?

____ percent

32. If you are required to contribute to your retirement plan in order to obtain the college or foundation contribution, what is the minimum percent of your annual base salary you must contribute?

____ percent

Miscellaneous

33. Would you be willing to share your contract/letter of agreement as part of this research (all identifiers will be eliminated).

☐ Yes   ☐ No

Additional comments:

34. Please share any clauses in your contract/letter of agreement which you feel are unique and beneficial for community college CEOs.

35. Please list any other concerns or issues relating to CEO contracts below.

General Information

35. How many years have you been employed in community colleges?

As president at this college	____ years
As president at other colleges	____ years
Total years in all community college positions	____ years

36. What is your age?

36. What is your sex?

☐ Male   ☐ Female

37. What is your race/ethnicity?

☐ White   ☐ African American   ☐ Hispanic

☐ Asian   ☐ Native American   ☐ Other

If you selected other, please specify:

38. What is the highest degree you have earned?

☐ Bachelor's   ☐ Master's   ☐ Doctorate

☐ JD or other Law degree   ☐ Other

If you selected other, please specify:

37. In what field did you earn your highest degree?

38. Please indicate any areas of specialized knowledge or expertise you have (e.g., learning college, finance, action research, international experience).

39. Please indicate, when applicable, the major field of your lower level degrees:

☐ Masters Degree   ☐ Baccalaureate   ☐ Associate Degree

☐ Other

References

American Association of Community Colleges. (2002). [CEO contract and compensation survey]. Unpublished raw data.

American Association of Community Colleges. (2005). *Recommended code of ethics for chief executive officers of community colleges.* Unpublished document.

American Association of Community Colleges. (2006). [CEO contract and compensation survey]. Unpublished raw data.

Association of Community College Trustees. (2007). *Standards of good practice for trustee boards.* Retrieved July 5, 2007, from www.acct.org/CenterEffectiveGoverna nce.asp?bid=89

Association of Governing Boards of Universities and Colleges. (2007). *AGB statement on board accountability.* Washington, DC: Author.

Association of Governing Boards Task Force on the State of the Presidency in American Higher Education. (2006). *The leadership imperative.* Washington, DC: Association of Governing Boards of Universities and Colleges.

Atwell, R. H., & Wellman, J. V. (2000). *Presidential compensation in higher education: Policies and best practices.* Washington, DC: Association of Governing Boards of Universities and Colleges.

Barwick J. (2002). Pathways to the presidency: Same trail, new vistas. *Community College Journal, 73*(1), 7–11.

Basinger, J. (2002, May 24). For presidents and boards, a handshake is no longer enough. *Chronicle of Higher Education, 48*(37), A29–A31.

Bornstein, R. (1998). In money matters, it's time for change. *Trusteeship, 6*(5), 4.

Burns, J. M. (1978). *Leadership.* New York: Harper & Row.

Campbell, D. F. (Ed.). (2002). *The leadership gap.* Washington, DC: Community College Press.

Community College Leadership Development Institute. (2001). *Preparing community college leaders for a new era* (Report No. 2). San Diego, CA: Mesa College Communications Services.

Cotton, R. D. (2002, July 26). Negotiating nonsalary benefits. *Chronicle of Higher Education, 48*(46).

Cotton, R. D. (2003, November 14). Negotiating your contract: Lessons from the front. *Chronicle of Higher Education, 50*(12), S36.

Davis, J. R. (2003). *Learning to lead.* Westport, CT: Praeger.

Davis, W. E., & Davis, D. (1999). The university presidency: Do evaluations make a difference? *Journal of Personnel Evaluation in Education, 12*(2), 119–140.

Fain, P. (2006). Dos and don'ts of writing presidential contracts. *Chronicle of Higher Education, 53*(14), 14b.

Gaskin, F. (1997). At the millennium. *New Directions for Community Colleges, 98,* 81–86.

Ingraham, M. H. (1968). *The mirror of brass: The compensation and working conditions of college and university administrators.* Madison: University of Wisconsin Press.

Ingram, R. T. (1997). Searching for reason in presidential compensation. *Trusteeship, 5*(4), 6–11.

Ingram, R. T., & Weary, W. A. (2000). *Presidential and board assessment in higher education: Purposes, policies and strategies.* Washington, DC: Association of Governing Boards of Universities and Colleges.

Jensen, R., Giles, R., & Kirklin, P. (2000). *Insider's guide to community college administration.* Washington, DC: Community College Press.

June, A. W. (2007). Presidents: Same look, different decade. *Chronicle of Higher Education, 53*(24), p. A3.

Kauffman, J. F. (1980). *At the pleasure of the board: The service of the college and university president.* Washington, DC: American Council on Education.

King, J. E. (2007). *The American college president:, 2007 edition.* Washington, DC: American Council on Education.

Nason, J. W. (1980). *The presidential search.* Washington, DC: Association of Governing Boards of Universities and Colleges.

Neff, C. B. (1993). Clear expectations. *Trusteeship, 1*(3), 20–23.

Nielsen, N., & Newton, W. (1997). Board–president relations: A foundation of trust. *New Directions for Community Colleges, 98,* 33–41.

Northouse, P. G. (2007). *Leadership: Theory and practice.* Thousand Oaks, CA: Sage.

Ottenritter, N. (2006). Competencies for community college leaders: The next step. *Community College Journal, 76*(4), 15–18.

Shults, C. (2001). *The critical impact of impending retirements on community college leadership* (Research Brief, Leadership Series No. 1). Washington, DC: American Association of Community Colleges.

Tranquada, R. E. (2001). *The compensation committee.* Washington, DC: Association of Governing Boards of Universities and Colleges.

Vaughan, G. B. (1992). *Dilemmas of leadership: Decision making and ethics in the community college.* San Francisco: Jossey-Bass.

Vaughan, G. B., & Weisman, I. M. (1998). *The community college presidency at the millennium.* Washington, DC: Community College Press.

Wallin, D. (2002). Professional development for presidents: A study of community and technical college presidents in three states. *Community College Review, 30*(2), 27–41.

Wallin, D. L. (Ed.). (2007). Ethical leadership: The role of the president. In D. M. Hellmich (Ed.), *Ethical leadership in the community college: Bridging theory and daily practice* (pp. 33–45). Bolton, MA: Anker Publishing.

Wallin, D., & Johnson, B. (2006). *Post-presidency pathways: Risk and reward.* Unpublished manuscript.

Wolin, C. (Ed.). (1996). *The CEO contract: Creating a winning partnership.* Washington, DC: Community College Press.

Zirkle, C., & Cotton, S. (2001). Where will future leadership come from? *Tech Directions, 61*(5), 15–18.

Index

About the Author

Desna L. Wallin is associate professor of adult education in the Department of Lifelong Education, Administration, and Policy at the University of Georgia. Before coming to the University of Georgia, she served for 6 years as president of Forsyth Technical Community College in Winston–Salem, North Carolina. Before her presidency in North Carolina, she served for 6 years as president of Clinton Community College in Clinton, Iowa. She has also been a member of the English faculty; dean of Transfer, General Studies and Developmental Programs; and vice president for Academic Affairs at Lincoln Land Community College in Springfield, Illinois. She began her career in community colleges as an adjunct faculty member.

Wallin has written numerous articles dealing with community college leadership, adjunct faculty, and professional development. She co-authored the book *Essentialism: Common Sense Quality Improvement;* edited and contributed chapters to the book *Adjunct Faculty in Community Colleges: An Academic Administrator's Guide to Recruiting, Supporting, and Retaining Great Teachers;* and wrote the first edition of *The CEO Contract: A Guide for Presidents and Boards.* She is a frequent presenter at regional, national, and international conferences and serves as a consultant to various professional organizations, colleges, and universities.

Wallin holds a BA in history from Brigham Young University, an MA in English education from Eastern Illinois University, and an EdD in postsecondary curriculum and instruction from Illinois State University.